Searching for Speech

"Here is a robust guide to a homiletics of entanglement that draws careful attention to the centrality of Earth in Scripture and in our lives. Sam Codington offers readers a profoundly honest approach, replete with rich examples, that begins and ends with the simple acknowledgement of our interdependence with all creation and celebrates in distinctive and particular ways as the world around us invites us to participate in the care and renewal of all forms of life."

—Paul Galbreath, Professor Emeritus of Theology, Union Presbyterian Seminary

"Sam Codington's *Searching for Speech* is a companion for any minister navigating the complexities of ecological crisis and faithful witness. His reflections on grief, entanglement, and transformation resonate deeply with my own journey of learning to walk more gently on the Earth. This book challenged me to rethink not just my sermons, but my relationships—with land, community, and the more-than-human world. It's a guide for leading with tenderness, truth, and hope."

—Sean Chow, Executive Director, Presbytery of San Diego

"People of all faiths and none carry deep experiences of the sacred in nature, along with growing anxiety about the escalating destruction of the natural world. From within this crucible, Sam Codington offers new 'language lessons' that give voice to the pain and fear, the possibility and reconnection that define this moment."

—Fletcher Harper, Executive Director, GreenFaith

"In the tradition of Wendell Berry, Sam Codington invites followers of Jesus to take seriously their relationship to the richness of the places they live, and to pay attention to even the tiny miracles of creation, like grass and snails and bees. But Codington locates the places he describes—and all creatures great and small—in the frame of epochal change, the Anthropocene. This makes for a challenging and especially helpful book. His commitment to childlike wonder—in himself and in others—is an inspiration, as are his tips for the practice of preaching in perilous times."

—John Fanestil, author of *American Heresy: The Roots and Reach of White Christian Nationalism*

Searching for Speech

Preaching in the Ruins of the Anthropocene

—⁂—

SAM CODINGTON

Foreword by
HyeRan Kim-Cragg

CASCADE Books · Eugene, Oregon

SEARCHING FOR SPEECH
Preaching in the Ruins of the Anthropocene

Copyright © 2026 Sam Codington. All rights reserved. Except for brief quotations in critical publications or reviews, no part of this book may be reproduced in any manner without prior written permission from the publisher. Write: Permissions, Wipf and Stock Publishers, 199 W. 8th Ave., Suite 3, Eugene, OR 97401.

Cascade Books
An Imprint of Wipf and Stock Publishers
199 W. 8th Ave., Suite 3
Eugene, OR 97401

www.wipfandstock.com

PAPERBACK ISBN: 979-8-3852-4148-4
HARDCOVER ISBN: 979-8-3852-4149-1
EBOOK ISBN: 979-8-3852-4150-7

Cataloguing-in-Publication data:

Names: Codington, Sam. | foreword by HyeRan Kim-Cragg.

Title: Searching for speech : preaching in the ruins of the Anthropocene / Sam Codington.

Description: Eugene, OR: Cascade Books, 2026 | Includes bibliographical references and index.

Identifiers: ISBN 979-8-3852-4148-4 (paperback) | ISBN 979-8-3852-4149-1 (hardcover) | ISBN 979-8-3852-4150-7 (ebook)

Subjects: LCSH: Ecotheology | Preaching | Theological anthropology—Christianity | Ecocriticism

Classification: BT695.5 C635 2026 (print) | BT695.5 (ebook)

*With gratitude for my dad,
the first preacher I heard*

Contents

Foreword by HyeRan Kim-Cragg | *xi*
Acknowledgments | *xv*

Introduction: Speechless in the Anthropocene | 1
    The Anthropocene: "The Human Dominated Epoch" | 3
    My Spiritual Heritage: A Pastor's Kid in the Presbyterian Church (USA) | 6
    A Way Ahead: Beginning Where It Hurts | 7
    My Ministry Context: San Diego/Tijuana Borderland | 9

CHAPTER 1: Feeding Capitalism's Hunger | 13
    Questions for reflection in preparation for this chapter—histories and proximity | 17
    Labor: Turning People into Objects for Consumption, Yesterday and Today | 17
    Land: Turning Places into Objects for Consumption, Yesterday and Today | 23
    Landfills: Turning Places into Sites for Waste, Yesterday and Today | 26
    Conclusions: We Have Normalized Desecration | 29
    Prompts for Preaching Preparation—Notice Where You Preach: | 31
    A Good Friday Sermon: "You Will Be With Me," Luke 23:43 | 32

CHAPTER 2: Witnessing Worlds Disappear | 34
    Questions for reflection in preparation for this chapter—witness and extinction | 36
    The Death of Relationship: Witnessing the Ravaged Relations within Forests | 37
    The Death of Childhood: Witnessing the Rapid Disappearance of Species | 40

Contents

The Death of Home: Witnessing Violence Against Indigenous
    Peoples | 43
The Death of Death: Practicing Resurrection with Trees
    and Local Communities | 46
Conclusion: Moving Beyond "Stewardship of Creation" | 49
Prompts for Preaching Preparation—Notice Human Impact | 51
Sermon: "Paying Attention, Facing Limits," Genesis 3:1–24 | 52
Sermon: "Reverence for Life," Romans 8:18–25 | 57

CHAPTER 3: Where to Begin? With Whom? | 62
    Questions for reflection in preparation for this chapter—
        Searching for Homiletical Guides | 66
    Where to Begin?: Taking an Inventory of "Here" | 66
    With Whom?: Working with Multiplicities of Wisdoms | 72
    Conclusions: Transformations of Being, Feeling, Seeing "Here" | 77
    Prompts for Preaching Preparation—Entering Community
        "Here": | 79
    Sermon: "In Deep Water," Jonah 1:17—2:10 | 79
    Sermon: "Learning to Weep: Loss, Lament, and Grief,"
        Luke 19:41–44 | 85

CHAPTER 4: Toward a Homiletics of Entanglement | 89
    Questions for reflection in preparation for this chapter—Practicing
        Homiletical Entanglement | 92
    Postcolonial Preaching: Creating a Subversive Event | 93
    Ecotheology: Listening with the Cry of the Earth | 96
    Postcolonial Ecotheology: Cultivating a Critical Consciousness | 99
    Biomimicry: Learning from the Genius of the Earth | 104
    Collective Effervescence: Moving Together with the Earth | 107
    Polyphonies: Attuning with Voices of the Earth | 109
    Conclusions: Finding Our Place(s) within the Earth | 112
    Prompts for Preaching Preparation—Cataloguing Embodied
        Entanglements: | 115
    Sermon: "Discovering Beautiful Entanglements," Ezekiel
        17:22–24 | 116

Conclusion: Friendship in the Garden 121
Bibliography | 125

Foreword

IN SEARCHING FOR SPEECH Sam Codington's tone is careful rather than boastful. He paints the world of preaching not so rosy. In fact, he is candid about the world being gloomy.

In a world of the Anthropocene, preaching should learn to speak of the language that expresses human grief, lament, anger, and despair in relationship with the Earth without losing sight of igniting hope and imbuing love, care, and joy.

Using a musical tone as an analogy, preaching addressing ecological issues should embrace playing with a minor key. If preaching is like forecasting difficult weather, it should be able to predict being cloudy rather than always proclaiming the glorious sunny days. That is what Codington does in this book.

"Are we preaching overconfident joy while the world weeps?" Codington asks, and notes that few Christians in the United States hear sermons addressing climate change and environmental catastrophe. He laments that many sermons do not hold the material life of a given place as substantial to and of theology and homiletics. "How can the Earth be our teacher so that our preaching arises from the life of the Earth?" he asks.

These self-reflective questions lead him to propose "a homiletics of entanglement," which is the work on homiletics connecting to ecology in ways that are confessional, self-conscious, and taking privileged preachers and congregation members' social locations seriously. By a homiletics of entanglement, he means a theory and practice of preaching that arises from local, biodiverse environments of a spiritual community in conversation with biblical texts.

Codington, as a white, male, educated person from the US, invites the readers who are identified as preachers to recognize themselves as the "beneficiaries of the global economy." Such an economy is so entangled and messed up that we must admit all are impacted by it, however

Foreword

differently. Hence, a theology of entanglement is most fitting for a homiletics of entanglement.

For preachers and churches, it remains fundamental to understand and unpack dynamics of power to analyze the impact in this human-dominated epoch of catastrophe.

While the entanglement of global economy is hard to grasp and may pose overwhelmingly heavy weight, Codington's personal and autobiographical examples are relatable, and accessible, especially his associations with trees in his childhood.

His personal stories are closely rooted in his own lived experiences yet very much resonate with many of our own experiences. Codington manages to include testimonials of the people around the world (including Canada, England, Brazil, Kenya, Thailand, and Korea), who disclose the precarious life due to the human greed and yet inspire us who hear their stories to move and act. These examples of lived experiences are powerful, as they communicate urgency and resiliency. They are effective sermon illustrations. Readers can see how Codington used these stories in his own preaching.

Urgency is the key word for this book, as the world in its biodiversity, is disappearing at the alarmingly fast speed, and therefore, the words that can address it must be appearing as urgently as possible, too. In fact, such words and such speech must be amplified in volume, and not just in speed. This amplification can be achieved by a homiletics of entanglement. Codington calls this preaching task the work of bearing witness to the world that is disappearing. The disappearing world of trees, moths, and so many other species results in the disappearing relationships, the loss of childhood, and the loss of home. And these losses are interconnected.

Codington brilliantly demonstrates this with urgency and in a serious tone, yet the overall message is faithful and hopeful, far from being depressing or despairing.

For me, one of the delights in reading this book was to discover how many earth-kin Codington uses to make his points. I decided to list a few here: ants, bees, beetles, butterflies, moths, dandelions, giant oak trees, tiny mosses, hummingbirds, crickets, kittens, algae, fungi, hickory forests, oceans, mountains, marshes, muds, mushrooms, tortoises, finches, rivers, meadow, creeks, coral reefs, grasses, lilies, ponds, seeds, soils, snails, and salmon.

Foreword

The multitude of earth-kin are our preaching partners and our preaching teachers. Codington's descriptions of them are contagious in delight and awe. Not only does he successfully amuse us with naming these multitude of species as our preaching partners and teachers, but he invites us to tap into other disciplines—novels, poetry, music—as sources of preaching imaginations and examples of preaching illustrations. Such a lavish homiletical invitation is in line with his extravagant inter- and cross-disciplinary attempts, incorporating postcolonial and eco-theological insights.

At the end, readers are in for treats as we can taste and see his spread. I want to call it a feast full of earthy and interdisciplinary preaching of entanglement that includes Codington's generous sharing of is own sermons.

Readers are encouraged and inspired by these sermons, guided by the biblical stories, ranging from the story in the garden of Eden, stories from the vision of Ezekiel, the teaching of the giant fish in the book of Jonah, the weeping Jesus in Luke, musings on Good Friday, and Paul's address of the creation groaning to the church in Rome.

Searching for Speech is a primer of homiletical entanglement, boldly proclaiming the gospel of the urgent need to engage climate crisis as faithful witness.

I am most grateful for Codington's passion, his practice, and his commitment to preaching climate crisis as fellow preacher, as teacher of preaching, and researcher of ecological preaching.

He is good company on my journey and I want to invite you all to join our journey for ecologically sound preaching.

HyeRan Kim-Cragg
Principal and Timothy Eaton Memorial Church Professor of Preaching
Emmanuel College, Toronto, Canada

Acknowledgments

SMALL SAPLINGS IN A forest draw their life from many places. The same is true of this book, and I am grateful.

Faith Presbyterian Church in the College Area of San Diego called me to be their pastor. I am grateful to have been their pastor from 2019 to 2024, and I am grateful for their care, support, and openness as I searched for the "sound of the genuine"[1] in me and the sound of the gospel among us.

The people of Border Church—including Rev. Dr. Seth Clark, Dr. John Fanestil, and Daniel Watman—have opened my eyes and heart to the manifold realities of the borderland of San Diego and Tijuana. When I was moderator of San Diego Presbytery, Dr. Fanestil invited me to participate in an ecumenical Good Friday service at Friendship Park in Tijuana, a service entitled "The Crucifixion of Friendship Park," gesturing towards the militarization of the border and the separation of migrant families. The people of Border Church have opened my heart to the wounds of the borderland. I express my deepest gratitude for their generous hospitality.

The Presbytery of San Diego, a network of relationships without which I would not have begun to feel the wounds of the borderland, elected me to serve as their moderator in 2023. While I was learning the procedures of Presbyterian Mid-Council polity, I was also encountering the beauty and challenges of ecumenical ministry, regionally and nationally. At the end of my term as presbytery moderator, we at Faith cherished the opportunity of hosting the presbytery's Leadership Day, for which we invited Dr. Cláudio Carvalhaes as our guest speaker.

Dr. Carvalhaes has encouraged and challenged me in my thinking like few people I have ever known. He has prompted me to feel and to think theologically as a thoroughly multidisciplinary practice, connecting insights from across diverse fields, including biology, fiction, memoir, poetry, sociology, theater, and postcolonial praxis. His play *When Wajcha Meets*

---

1. Thurman, "Sound of the Genuine."

Acknowledgments

Pachamama embodies this sense of feeling the world in a multidisciplinary mode, as the play explores climate disaster from the perspective of a clown. For sharing his theological imagination with me, I owe him a debt I will never be able to repay.

My profound gratitude goes to Dr. HyeRan Kim-Cragg for her scholarship and support of this book. Her connections between homiletics and Anthropocene studies are an inspiration for me.

Throughout my time in San Diego, I met weekly with Rev. Megan Cochran, Rev. Kim Dawsey-Richardson, and Rev. Nathan Byrd to discuss church life and the ministry of preaching. If it was not for them, I do not know whether I would have survived as a preacher more than a few months. Rev. Jeya So and Rev. Liz Wilson-Manahan joined the fray of weekly preaching conversations and enriched my life as a result. I am grateful for their friendship as colleagues in ministry.

My parents, Herb and Suzan, nurtured my childhood imagination with steady rivers of prayer, preaching, and stories. If they had not raised me on a small farm in South Carolina, I do not know whether I would feel the same way about the Earth as I do now. I am grateful to them for allowing me to roam freely among the trees for endless hours.

I am grateful to the trees of my childhood—the cedars, maples, oaks, and pines, who populated my childhood imagination and made a home for me. I realize consciously now more than I ever have that the trees of my childhood have been and continue to be my professors of theology, liturgy, and homiletics. I write this book in gratitude to them, and I hope my life will offer some modest contribution to their well-being.

I could hardly write a word without Esther and Ezra. While writing this book, on occasion, I turned to Esther and asked questions, such as, "How will my sermon change if I hold hands with a tree as I am preparing the sermon? What is the smell of a sermon?" Esther and Ezra are my heart.

Introduction
Speechless in the Anthropocene

> "Climate change is a global problem... Its worst
> impact will probably be felt by developing
> countries in the coming decades."[1]
>
> POPE FRANCIS

> "Climate change alone, if left unabated,
> could be the primary cause of extinction
> of a quarter of the species of plants and animals
> on the land by midcentury."[2]
>
> E. O. WILSON

> "If current trends continue, we will not.
> And that is qualitatively and epochally true.
> If religion does not speak to [this],
> it is an obsolete distraction."[3]
>
> DANIEL MAGUIRE

---

1. Pope Francis, *Laudato Si': On Care for Our Common Home*, 21–22. As they consider the many layers of human tragedies in the twenty-first century, Tsing, Deger, Saxena, and Zhou wonder whether ethnographers may also consider intersections of popular culture, asking, "Where and how does climate emerge in popular culture, like the lyrics of *norteña* ballads, or Spanish hip-hop? How is the pope's encyclical on climate change being interpreted in sermons of local Catholic churches?" *Field Guide to the Patchy Anthropocene*, 90.

2. Wilson, *Creation*, 74.

3. As cited by Rasmussen in *Earth Communities, Earth Ethics*, 10.

Searching for Speech

> "*The* moral issue of our day—and
> the vocation to which we are called—
> is whether we and other species
> will live and how well we will live."[4]
>
> Sallie McFague

When I was a young child, perhaps five years old, I arranged my siblings' stuffed animals on a couch in the living room of my parents' farmhouse, and I preached to them. They were my first congregation. I drew inspiration, no doubt, from witnessing my dad preach, as I sent paper airplanes sailing through the church sanctuary. I have been searching for preaching words ever since, though I have also spent much of my life attempting to escape the vocation of preaching, like Jonah in the Old Testament, with his feet moving in one direction and his heart pulling him in the opposite direction. I was a teenager the first time I delivered a sermon in the context of a church worship service. I was immensely overconfident as I preached from a sermon outline scrawled on wrinkled notebook paper. More than twenty years have passed. Since being ordained as a pastor in the Presbyterian Church (USA), I have been given the gift and responsibility of preaching in varied settings, from small towns and rural communities to suburbs and urban centers. Repeatedly, through oftentimes perplexing experiences, I have found myself drawn to the preaching life as my life's calling, though admittedly I feel far less confident now than when I preached that first sermon. Now, I have found myself at loss for words.

The times in which we live are absurd. Contradiction defines our days. Multitudes of people go hungry while multitudes of people throw away food. Countless children suffer digging for cobalt for rechargeable batteries while countless children suffer from loneliness as they recharge their smartphones. Slavery has been outlawed across the world while modern slavery is more profitable than ever before. Laws dictate nearly every corner of our lives in the West while Black men are killed in the street by white vigilantes. Western countries profess allegiance to a poor Palestinian Jew named Jesus of Nazareth while Western countries shut out refugees at our national borders. Cities across the world experience high levels of unhealthy air quality while forests across the world are bulldozed to feed the lifestyles of cities. It is as if we have located the mythic Tree of Life and are setting it aflame.

---

4. McFague, *Body of God*, 9.

Introduction

What possibly can be said in a time of enormous wastefulness, mass extinctions, climate change, climate refugees, and rapacious extractivism? I am writing this book to search for a response to that question. Many days, as I have the responsibility of preparing sermons, I feel that our times are beyond speech and can be accompanied only by "sighs too deep for words," as the apostle Paul wrote in the New Testament Letter to the Romans.[5] Yet, preachers have a responsibility to speak and to speak truthfully. It is from a place of speechlessness in the face of manifold calamities that a preacher, empowered by the Spirit, speaks.[6]

THE ANTHROPOCENE: "THE HUMAN DOMINATED EPOCH"

With the wide-ranging impacts of climate change, I am unconvinced that many of us speak in ways that are attuned to the times and places in which we live, and more importantly, I am unconvinced that many of us speak in ways that are attuned to the life of the Earth. Or, as Rev. Otis Moss III has asserted, "America is living stormy Monday, but the pulpit is preaching happy Sunday. The world is experiencing the Blues, but pulpiteers are dispensing excessive doses of non-prescribed prosaic sermons with severe

---

5. Romans 8:26, NRSV. Justo L. González and Catherine G. González argue, "One can only know injustice when one suffers it. The word of the gospel today, as in the times of Jesus, as ever, comes to us most clearly in the painful groans of the oppressed. We must listen to those groans. We join the struggle to the point where we too must groan. Or we may choose the alternative, which is not to hear the gospel at all." *Liberating Pulpit*, 65.

6. It is not by a colossal or Sisyphean effort of one's own that a preacher speaks but by the Spirit, as Luke A. Powery proclaims, "the wind, the breath of the Spirit, blows through multiplicity and polyphony." *Becoming Human*, 88. Gustavo Gutierrez observed, "The historical starting point for the following of Jesus and for reflection on this following is to be found in the experience that comes from the Spirit." *We Drink from Our Own Wells*, 5. Jürgen Moltmann noted, "The experience of the Spirit is the reason for the eschatological longing for the completion of salvation, the redemption of the body and the new creation of all things. Impelled by the Spirit, Christians cry, 'Maranatha, come, Lord Jesus!' (Rev. 22:20). It is the experience of the Spirit which makes Christians in every society restless and homeless, and on the search for the kingdom of God (Heb. 13:14), for it is this experience of God which makes them controvert and contravene a godless world of violence and death. The Spirit makes them rich in experience and rich in hope, but poor and lonely in a world gone wrong. The cry for the coming of the Spirit takes up out of the depths of the cries of the dumb, and brings them before God. In praying for the coming of the Spirit, men and women open themselves for his coming." *Spirit of Life*, 73–74.

ecclesiastical and theological side effects."[7] Are we preaching overconfident joy while the world weeps? Few Christians in the United States hear sermons addressing climate change and environmental catastrophe. In 2022, between 63 and 81 percent of Christians in the United States—Mainline Protestant, Historically Black Protestant, Evangelical, Roman Catholic—reported hearing few or no sermons addressing climate change and the environment. Even fewer congregants reported speaking about climate change and environmental catastrophe with other congregants.[8] Most preachers are not addressing what Sallie McFague said is "*the* moral issue of our day," and we are not equipping our congregations to do so either.

In my search for speech, I am focusing not only on the art of preaching itself but on the theology and historical positioning of a preacher in relation to the Earth. The theology and historical positioning of a preacher will invariably inform the art and substance of preaching, the focus and function of sermons. Most fundamentally, I am asking, "How can the Earth be our teacher so that our preaching arises from the life of the Earth?"

Modern Western society has written histories from an exclusively human and most often white male perspective of time. Widespread species extinctions, soil erosion, rising ocean acidity, and climate change accentuate the importance of counting time in geologic time, rather than only in human time. Moving against the common currents of Western individualism and anthropocentrism, the present moment requires a broader, more entangled view of history and time and place, interpreting human society as within "nature."[9] This will require a shift in perspective, from understanding humans as over the Earth's ecosystems to understanding humans as within the Earth's ecosystems.[10]

The Anthropocene is what many scientists are calling the epoch we have now entered, in which the impact of humans and our exponential growth rising from colonial and industrial projects shape the future of the entire planet.[11] This is new territory. We have left the geological epoch of

---

7. Moss III, *Blue Note Preaching in a Post-Soul World*, 4.
8. Alper, "How Religion Intersects with Americans' Views on the Environment."
9. Rasmussen, *Earth Community, Earth Ethics*, 34.
10. Boff, *Cry of the Earth, Cry of the Poor*, xii.
11. Though an international science committee decided not to designate the current epoch "the Anthropocene" in 2024, Tsing, Deger, Saxena, and Zhou comment, "The term 'Anthropocene' has been much criticized—and often rightly so—for what it omits as well as what it misleadingly emphasizes. Yet Anthropocene has become a gathering point for discussion of environmental dangers, across disciplines and political divisions, and this

Introduction

the Holocene behind. The Dutch chemist Paul Crutzen created the word *Anthropocene* to describe the "human-dominated, geological epoch." Crutzen observed that humans have significantly altered the Earth's atmosphere with a combination of deforestation and fossil fuel combustion, increasing carbon dioxide in the air by 40 percent in the last two centuries.[12] The Anthropocene is the human-dominated epoch.

Leonardo Boff described the current epoch most vividly: "We have inaugurated a new geological age, the Anthropocene: in other words, the human being is a hurtling meteor capable of decimating the Earth."[13] For the present work, the Anthropocene will be the context for practicing theology and understanding the historical positioning of a preacher in relation with the Earth. Hyeran Kim-Cragg notes the importance of the Anthropocene for the field of homiletics, as she writes, "A creation centered approach to preaching helps to ground us in the urgent concern of the Anthropocene age when environmental exploitation and the consumption of fossil fuels threaten our very existence. Postcolonial theologians seek to articulate 'planetary loves,' humbly acknowledging that humans are only a small species, rather than the center of the universe."[14] Kim-Cragg's connections between homiletics, postcolonial praxis, and the Anthropocene are vital for the present work.

As we acknowledge and engage this human-dominated epoch of calamity, we should be careful, however, not to assume that all humans are impacting and being impacted in the same and equal ways. Elizabeth M. DeLoughrey has observed that discourses engaging the Anthropocene sometimes describe an "undifferentiated man" as the instigator of environmental catastrophe. "These environmental morality tales," DeLoughrey explains, "are, of course, allegories of a universal masculine subject who is not subject to cultural, historical, or sexual difference. When Anthropocene journalists insist that the term 'man' is gender neutral, it seems as if the decades of work about context and difference in the humanities never existed."[15] For preachers and churches, identity and social location

---

seems to us a good enough reason to use it. Perhaps the one feature of the Anthropocene on which most commentators agree is its planetary nature: From climate change to the extinction crisis, and from radioactivity to industrial toxins, this is not a local storm." *Field Guide to the Patchy Anthropocene*, 23.

12. Kolbert, *Sixth Extinction*, 107–8.
13. Boff, *Thoughts and Dreams of an Old Theologian*, 93.
14. Kim-Cragg, *Postcolonial Preaching*, 22.
15. DeLoughrey, *Allegories of the Anthropocene*, 11.

of particular individuals, communities, and places remain fundamental for understanding dynamics of power and impact in this human-dominated epoch of catastrophe. The Anthropocene, then, may not be understood as a singular totality, but rather as a violently variegated patchwork of desecrations and wastelands, with imbalances of impact and responsibility—a teenage female Congolese artisanal miner does not experience the desecration of her homeland in the same or even similar ways as an older male British naturalist.[16]

Throughout the body of this text, I use the first-person plural pronoun "we." First and foremost, I am addressing preachers, church leaders, church insiders such as church members, and leaders of spiritual communities. Second, I am addressing those of us who are beneficiaries of a globalized economy that exploits and devours the planet, admittedly "we" and "us" will continue to be fluid and porous. I hope this vision of "we" will become clearer in chapter 1. By using the first-person plural pronoun "we," I am offering a critique of our historical positioning in the Western church and an invitation into a broader and deeper way of relating and being entangled with the life of the Earth. "We" is a shorthand address to all of us who, in varying ways, profess a commitment to care for the Earth and are responsible for its destruction.

For the present work, the focus will not involve debates about how to analyze or interpret environmental data. The focus here will involve exploring ways for preachers, spiritual leaders, and church leaders to speak with their communities about the time and place in which we live. I am unconvinced whether we have speech to articulate the tragedies encircling us every day. What follows is my search for speech during the Anthropocene.

MY SPIRITUAL HERITAGE: A PASTOR'S KID IN THE PRESBYTERIAN CHURCH (USA)

Long before I read Jürgen Moltmann's *The Crucified God,* I heard my dad preaching sermons describing the suffering of Jesus on the cross. My dad was the first preacher I witnessed on a regular basis. His most impactful sermons on my young theological imagination focused on Jesus' suffering

---

16. Tsing, Deger, Saxena, and Zhou stress this point, asserting, "It is impossible to describe the Anthropocene without regard for the fundamentally unequal relations among humans through which environmental effects of the human presence are structured." *Field Guide to the Patchy Anthropocene,* 26–27.

INTRODUCTION

and our responsibility to "serve the underserved." He grew up as the oldest child of Presbyterian medical missionaries in Korea. His mother was a nurse and his father was a medical doctor, who developed a reputation for providing medical treatment among Korea's and Bangladesh's poorest communities. His father's example influenced his worldview just as his preaching has influenced mine.

Mainline Protestantism has been the context in which I have been nurtured as a preacher. The Presbyterian Church (USA) has been and continues to be my spiritual home. I have drawn inspiration for my preaching from the writings of Karl Barth, Walter Brueggemann, Archbishop Desmond Tutu, and Serene Jones. Karl Barth led me to see the preacher as witness. Walter Brueggemann showed me how to encounter the contemporaneity of biblical texts as few people have. Archbishop Desmond Tutu revealed to me how to embody joy in the face of calamity. Serene Jones lives with an incarnational and courageous prophetic vision. I owe much to their wisdom and practice of preaching. Moreover, the Presbyterian Church (USA) has included climate change as one of its "intersectional priorities" related to its Matthew 25 initiative. This attention to climate change and environmental racism is nothing new for the PC(USA). It has regularly acknowledged global warming's impact especially on "the least of these" since the early 1980s, when the environmental justice movement was in its infancy.[17] This church context has nurtured and inspired my faith as a vocation of action in the world. I owe much to this denomination and to the preachers who have challenged my theological imagination.

While my theological imagination has been formed from an early age by a "preferential option for the poor," I have felt a growing intuition that many of us are speaking as if we are contemporaries of John Calvin in the sixteenth century, when there were hardly more than four hundred million humans occupying the entire planet. If our preaching sounds as if it belongs in an era other than our own, perhaps in the 1640s or 1950s or 1980s, it probably does. We need new speech for today.

A WAY AHEAD: BEGINNING WHERE IT HURTS

After writing at the intersection of liturgy, colonization, and white supremacy,[18] I felt a gnawing awareness that the world as we have known

---

17. See Presbyterian Mission, "Intersectional Priority."
18. Codington, *Listening as Hosts*.

it is disappearing but few people in my fields of preaching, liturgy, and theology are talking about it within the context of local churches. Initially, I was not sure what to make of the scarcity of discourse and praxis. The world as we have known it has ended before, most recently with the COVID-19 pandemic. The world ends at the beginning of every war. The world ends every time an old growth forest is bulldozed for cash crops. The world has ended many times before. It is ending again, but this time is different.

Others, such as Phyllis Tickle, have written books about the cyclical character of broad-scale change. In *The Great Emergence*, Tickle traced what she called a "rummage sale" that occurs in religion and society every 500 years. Cyclical interpretations of history offer reassurances that what is happening now has happened before. This offers the consolation that while changes may be hard, they are survivable. However, Tickle does not speak at all in *The Great Emergence* about environmental catastrophes. So, how do we speak of rapidly disappearing topsoil, insects, birds, old-growth forests, and coral reefs? In other words, how do we speak of change when the devastating changes that are occurring are not the undoing of hundreds of years but of millions of years?[19] Moreover, what do we say when the changes we are facing now are not cyclical and have not been faced by our species before? Thomas Berry describes the unique quality of our current situation, as he observes,

> We are experiencing a disintegration of the life systems of the planet just when the Earth in the diversity and resplendence of its self-expression had attained a unique grandeur. This moment deserves special attention on the part of humans who are themselves bringing about this disintegration in a manner that has never happened previously in the entire 4.6 billion years of Earth history.[20]

As Berry observes, we are not facing cyclical changes. We are in the midst of disintegration that is unique and has not been caused previously by a single species in Earth's history.

For manifold reasons, then, I have a gnawing suspicion that we preachers need to reassess the field of preaching, beginning where it hurts.[21] In chapter 1, "Feeding Capitalism's Hunger," I reexamine our historical

---

19. Rob Nixon describes the challenge of narrating what he calls "slow violence" that happens gradually and out of sight and is dispersed across time. *Slow Violence and the Environmentalism of the Poor*, 2.

20. Berry, *Great Work*, 49.

21. James Cone as cited by Carvalhaes in *Ritual at World's End*, 25.

INTRODUCTION

positioning. Are we preachers fully accommodated to empire's predatory economics devouring the Earth? In chapter 2, "Witnessing Worlds Disappear," I follow four variegated narratives that draw long-term devastations into view. Are we in relationship with the places in which we live in order to notice the vast mistreatment and disappearances of biodiverse ecosystems? In chapter 3, "Where to Begin? With Whom?," I offer a shift in genealogies of authorization. Who are our homiletical authorities? In chapter 4, "Toward A Homiletics of Entanglement," I offer an interdisciplinary homiletical theology and methodology, drawing together postcolonial preaching and ecological theology. What is animating our theology as we write and preach sermons? I attempt to draw together these inquiries in the form of six sermons. I include one sermon at the end of chapters 1 and 4, and I include two sermons at the end of chapters 2 and 3. I am continuing to ask, "What is the sound of good news in the Anthropocene arising from my voice?"

I am asking these questions as a parish pastor who has been preaching on a weekly basis for more than a decade and who holds in view the daily lives of beloved people in the congregation and the surrounding community. Many of the pressing issues in the Anthropocene can feel enormous and far afield from the daily lives of people with whom I preach, teach, support, lead, and live. Drawing into focus the pressing issues of the Anthropocene as practically integrated within all of our lives will be an important element in my search for speech.

MY MINISTRY CONTEXT:
SAN DIEGO/TIJUANA BORDERLAND

Though I have preached in congregations in rural areas, farming communities, textile mill communities, and small towns, I wrote this book in a city, in the College Area of San Diego, adjacent with the main entrance of San Diego State University, a neighborhood bustling with students, faculty, staff, unhoused neighbors, and young families with preschool children.

I worked through many of the questions in this book as a parish pastor, who preached on weekly basis in a vortex of harsh realities, education, and entertainment in San Diego. I have been encircled by the mistreatment of refugees at the US/Mexico border, the energy of college students, and the allure of San Diego's tourism industry. News reports that describe the inhumane detainment of refugees and the erecting of thirty-foot walls unfold only seventeen miles from where I preach each Sunday. Countless college students regularly saunter through the church campus between classes and parties. I often speak with them over a cup of coffee or a slice of pizza. Concerts and events that celebrate human artistic achievement often happen less than a half a mile away from where I preach each Sunday. Admittedly, preaching does not happen only in a pulpit and on a Sunday morning. Nonetheless, the weekly worship liturgy and formal homily emerge in this vortex of harsh realities, education, and entertainment.

Our daily lives in the College Area of San Diego unfold in what is a fragile coastal desert, which draws the vast majority of its water from elsewhere in order to maintain the lifestyles of the city. Kumeyaay peoples have loved and lived on this land for thousands of years. Any attunement with the land will need to include attunement with the peoples who love the land and who have been forcibly displaced.

In the disclosing process of unlearning and relearning to preach encircled by catastrophe, I desire to feel and to speak from and within the places I occupy. I have traced previously ways we in the West presume to be the host wherever we are, though the Earth has always been the actual host.[22] In this book, I am seeking to unlearn my disregard for our true host, the Earth. My search for speech during the Anthropocene has been a journey, and much of the time, I have been taking steps without knowing what I was doing or even attempting to do. As Thomas Merton said, "I have no idea where I am going. I do not see the road ahead of me."[23]

As I have sketched stories, preached sermons, and shared conversations, I have been surprised by people's regular and meaningful responses of gratitude. Visitors and church members have continually expressed their appreciation for my humble efforts at speaking about our responsibility and relationship with the Earth. On one occasion in particular, a church member expressed her gratitude after a worship service with tears streaking down her cheeks, saying, "I love your sermons about caring for the Earth," and on the following day, a visitor called the church and told me on the phone, "I am a Christian and go to large churches, but I do not hear people talking about the environment. I am glad you are. We need to be talking about our relationship with the Earth." I share this only to encourage preachers that, while there will likely always be detractors, you may be surprised by people's heartfelt desire to learn more about how Christian faith calls us to

---

22. Codington, *Listening as Hosts*.
23. Merton, "Merton Prayer."

INTRODUCTION

be in mutual relationship with the Earth. I have been happily surprised by how many people respond with a desire to (un)learn and to act, and I am increasingly convinced that part of a preacher's role during the Anthropocene is to experiment with language for talking about our grief, lament, anger, love, joy, despair, and hope in relationship with the Earth. I believe a pastor's ongoing experimentation with language and stories amidst the Anthropocene will offer congregations widening and deepening capacities for expressing themselves in their own search for speech during this time and place of catastrophe.

CHAPTER 1

Feeding Capitalism's Hunger

"We are literally consuming our planet."[1]

ELLEN F. DAVIS

"Almost all tropical deforestation is driven
by demand for four commodities: beef, soy,
palm oil, and wood. Beef cattle are responsible
for more than double the deforestation of the other
three combined. In the Amazon, providing
land for beef cattle to graze on is directly
responsible for more than 80 percent of
the deforestation."[2]

CHRISTIANA FIGUERES

"You shall no longer give the people straw
to make bricks, as before;
let them go and gather straw for themselves.
But you shall require of them
the same quantity of bricks."

EXODUS 5:7–8

TREES TOWERED OVER ME as a child in rural South Carolina. I grew to know the shade and barks and smells of cedars, maples, oaks, and pines. But I knew nothing of old growth forests. That would not come until much later.

1. Davis, "Knowing Our Place on Earth," 61.
2. Figueres and Rivett-Carnac, *Future We Choose*, 124.

I knew almost only forests that were regularly harvested for pulpwood or cleared for cattle grazing. Every few decades, rotating plots of pines around our miniature farm would be cut down and new saplings would begin to emerge from the bulldozed soil. As a child, I did not comprehend that the mechanisms of capitalistic consumerism shaped my childhood landscapes, though we were hours of driving in a car from any city. The current use of land rises from a history of land theft and the emergence of modern consumerism. As a child in rural South Carolina, the planting and cutting of trees felt as familiar to me as the four seasons. I could not have imagined at the time that the bulldozed landscapes surrounding my home were a mild expression of what Western countries do to many countries around the world.

White supremacist colonization has uprooted peoples from lands, turning peoples and lands into commodities for profit. Capitalism has become the economic system for white supremacy, while white supremacy has become the aesthetic and logic for neocolonial capitalism.[3] Anna Lowenhaupt Tsing notes, "In capitalist logics of commodification, things are torn from their life-worlds to become objects of exchange."[4] Seen with this historical lens, wealth and land use are not neutral or amoral. In the Anthropocene, we humans are destroying each other and our own home, the Earth, while seeking ceaselessly to widen profit margins without concern for the loss of biodiversity and the long-term consequences to local communities. Leonardo Boff has expressed this unfolding reality succinctly.

> The logic that exploits classes and subjects peoples to the interests of a few rich and powerful countries is the same logic as the logic that devastates the Earth and plunders its wealth, showing no solidarity with the rest of humankind and future generations.[5]

Boff connects the exploitation of people and land. They are not separate realities. When we speak of the treatment of peoples and communities, we must also speak of the treatment of land. Gordon Aeschliman has commented, "Here's the harsh reality of the poor: it is usually their resources that we [in the US] are capturing to support our lifestyle, and their lands, rivers, and lakes are where we are dumping our waste."[6] Aeschliman continues,

---

3. I explored this history briefly in *Listening as Hosts*.
4. Tsing, *Mushroom at the End of the World*, 121.
5. Boff, *Cry of the Earth, Cry of the Poor*, xi.
6. Aeschliman, "Loving the Earth is Loving the Poor," 92.

> In the wealthy West, we live what is called a "phantom" lifestyle. Rather than relying on the earth around us, we almost invisibly (like a phantom) rely on the earth of others. If we run out of vegetables, we import them from another country. If we need more electricity, we import it from another state or river or region. The same is true of water, minerals, fruit, and meat. If we need more petroleum, we import it from abroad.[7]

Because we do not see on a daily basis where the materials we use come from or where they go after we are finished using them, we do not see the devastating cost to the Earth and to the people whose communities have been plundered to support our lifestyles in the West. Aeschliman notes, "The true cost of living the modern lifestyle is not measured by what we pay at the cash register. Rather, it is measured by what we have done to other people's rivers, valleys, oceans, and land. And, more precisely, what we have done to the poor."[8] We in the West are living a phantom lifestyle, exploiting the land and labor of people we will likely never meet.[9]

Though the brutal treatment of Indigenous peoples in the Amazon rainforest and peoples in the Democratic Republic of the Congo should not be compared to economically depressed communities in the United States, it is worth noting that we in the West are not hurting and plundering communities only in other countries. We are doing this to our own land, people, and communities. Wendell Berry draws into focus how agribusiness has displaced people in farming communities in the United States. With the development of more expensive farming technologies and the expectation that small farms must grow exponentially larger in order to compete, many small farms have closed, leading Berry to observe, "What we have called agricultural progress has, in fact, involved the forcible displacement of millions of people."[10] We in the United States are hurting communities not

---

7. Aeschliman, "Loving the Earth is Loving the Poor," 93.
8. Aeschliman, "Loving the Earth is Loving the Poor," 93–94.
9. Justo L. González and Catherine G. González observe that those living a seemingly comfortable middle-class life are part of a system of bondage: "If we can become aware of the social, political, and economic systems that control our lives, we may then find ourselves on the same side of the struggle as those who are outcasts of those systems," and they continued, "Once we have acknowledged our own lack of freedom, we can find ourselves learning much about our own struggle from those whom we charitably tried to help before. They can become our teachers, rather than we theirs. The poor, precisely because they are at the margins of the system, may well know more about its actual working than we who are kept within it." *Liberating Pulpit*, 28.
10. Berry, *Unsettling of America*, 45.

only in other countries; we are also hurting communities and citizens of our own country.

The exploitation of people and land are connected by the same logic. Moreover, we should be careful not to separate diverse species, the human and the more-than-human. Larry Rasmussen describes the practice of separating species as "the apartheid habit of distinguishing 'human' from 'nonhuman,'"[11] treating humans as the only species worthy of moral consideration. However, many species, including humans, contribute to creating biodiverse ecosystems on which the Earth's life depends. Therefore, the cost of exploiting peoples and lands should not be measured, interpreted, or articulated only by the cost to human communities, but by the cost to all diverse species who constitute an ecosystem. As Wendell Berry has asserted, "Our bodies . . . are not distinct from the bodies of plants and animals, with which we are involved in the cycles of feeding and in the intricate companionships of ecological systems of the spirit. They are not distinct from the earth, the sun and moon, and other heavenly bodies."[12] The human and the more-than-human all constitute biodiverse communities that contribute to the life of the Earth, and all are worthy of moral consideration.

Preaching during the Anthropocene will need to be deeply attuned and will need to express the interconnected relations across lands and communities of the human and the more-than-human. While the positions and relations of preachers within environmental catastrophes vary—an Anglo-American female preacher in a suburb of Atlanta and a Puerto Rican male preacher in Tijuana will experience environmental catastrophes differently—their urgency and attunement should persist with passion and resolve.

At the end of this chapter, I include prompts for preaching preparation, and I offer a Good Friday sermon/poem. This Good Friday sermon/poem turns on positioning and proximity, the proximity of Jesus, the preacher, the congregation, and the devastations of the Earth in the wake of capitalism's hunger. Jesus is with the devastated ones. In preparing for this Good Friday sermon, I asked, "Where am I and where is my congregation in relation to these devastations? How can we close the distance between the devastations and ourselves?" This chapter may prove most useful by reading the sermon at the end of the chapter first, reading the chapter, and then rereading the sermon again.

---

11. Rasmussen, *Earth Community, Earth Ethics*, 32.
12. Berry, *Unsettling of America*, 107.

In order to vivify the link between the logic that exploits people and plunders the land, I trace historical realities of labor, land, and landfills. The purpose here is not to be exhaustive but rather to draw attention to a preacher's historical positioning and proximity. While doing so, I want to raise a question: "Are we preachers in the West acclimated to empire's predatory economics destroying the Earth? In what ways can our preaching at least begin to witness and articulate our participation and responsibility within a predatory economy?" In the Anthropocene, we humans are consuming each other and our own home, the Earth. Consuming and destroying each other and the Earth has a history that shapes the present, and to that history we will now turn.

QUESTIONS FOR REFLECTION IN PREPARATION FOR THIS CHAPTER—HISTORIES AND PROXIMITY

What are histories of exploited land, labor, and landfills in the area where I live?

What is my proximity with the devastations of exploited land, labor, and landfills?

What is the proximity of my spiritual community's gathering space/church campus/sanctuary in relation with these devastations?

What are products I regularly use that are results from exploited land and labor and where are those products disposed when I am finished with them?

In what ways might my sermons articulate and embody distance and/or closeness with these devastations?

In what ways do I/we see Jesus in relation with these devastations?

LABOR: TURNING PEOPLE INTO OBJECTS FOR CONSUMPTION, YESTERDAY AND TODAY

Enslaved African peoples were the labor force on which the United States was built. Many of us may want to assume that the brutality of enslavement is a matter of past history and has little if any bearing on our lives today, but the exploitative labor practices of capitalism that shape our lives today grew from the capitalist economy dependent on enslaved people. The past is ever-present.

Sven Beckert and Seth Rockman have charted connections between the histories of enslavement and capitalism in the United States. Slavery and capitalism are intertwined. Beckert and Rockman observe "that slave-grown cotton was the most valuable export made in America, that the capital stored in slaves exceeded the combined value of all the nation's railroads and factories, that foreign investment underwrote the expansion of plantation lands in Louisiana and Mississippi, that the highest concentration of steam power in the United States was to be found along the Mississippi rather than on the Merrimack."[13] And they continue, "American slavery is necessarily imprinted on the DNA of American capitalism."[14] They show that slavery was not a regional reality limited to the South. Rather, slavery and the economic benefits of slavery flowed through every financial institution in the United States and abroad. As slavery's capitalism reduced people to "units of exchange,"[15] slavery expanded beyond the plantation and into finance in the North, national institutions, and international markets.

On the plantations in the South, enslavers sought to increase efficiency in order to increase production and widen profit margins. "Between 1790 and 1860," Edward E. Baptist notes, "more land, a vast and highly capitalized slave trade, punishment, increased surveillance, decreased breaks, and lockstep labor . . . made possible a vast increase in the number of cotton plants being tended in the United States. The amount of cotton produced in the United States grew from 20 million pounds around 1805 . . . to over two billion pounds of cotton in 1860, an increase of 10,000 percent."[16] Brutality enabled increases in profits, or as Baptist observes, "The whip made cotton. And whip-made increases in the efficiency of picking had global significance. They pushed down the real price of cotton, which by 1860 had fallen to one quarter of its 1800 price, even as demand had increased many times over."[17] Enslavers wielded unspeakable violence to widen profit margins.

In the world of finance, enslavers acquired mortgages in order to purchase enslaved people. Bonnie Martin writes, "Thousands of southerners sold and bought slaves on installment plans secured by mortgages," and she notes, "The earliest slave mortgages in Louisiana date from the French

---

13. Beckert and Rockman, *Slavery's Capitalism*, 1–2.
14. Beckert and Rockman, *Slavery's Capitalism*, 3.
15. Beckert and Rockman, *Slavery's Capitalism*, 11.
16. Cited in Beckert and Rockman, *Slavery's Capitalism*, 40.
17. Cited in Beckert and Rockman, *Slavery's Capitalism*, 52.

period, at least as early as 1738."[18] Enslaved people were also used as a means of acquiring mortgages in order to purchase land, agricultural machinery, and social status. Martin comments, "Of the total amount of capital raised by equity mortgages, the percentage of capital raised by those using human collateral was the same in both Virginia and Louisiana during their early frontier eras: in each colony more than two-thirds of the capital lent was backed by a borrower pledging slaves as all or part of the security for the loan."[19] Humans were reduced to units of exchange in order to build purchasing power and expand profits.

Considering the involvement of international markets with the slave economy, Kathryn Boodry has examined the "entangled relationship of state-charted banks, government-issued bonds, and remote investors in Europe and the northern United States."[20] The pervasiveness of the slave economy was far reaching. Boodry explains, "The fact of the matter is that, in the nineteenth century, involvement in the American trade, whether in goods produced for commercial sale or in financial instruments such as bonds, meant involvement in some fashion with slave labor."[21] Eric Kimball has considered specifically ways in which New Englanders "depended on slave labor plantation regimes of the West Indies to purchase their exports." And Kimball notes, "New Englanders supported the plantation regimes in the Caribbean by supplying critical infrastructure elements like oil, candles, fish, livestock, and wood. To carry these commodities, New Englanders built a vast maritime fleet and employed locals to crew their ships."[22] Across international markets, from Charleston to Liverpool and London, no one was free from the moral stain of slavery's capitalism. John Majewski has gone so far as to observe that "slavery . . . stood at the center of the world's capitalist economy."[23]

Not only did the labor of enslaved people of African descent physically build the United States, but all the financial systems of this country were built by exploiting and exchanging their forced labor. In the past, none of the world was free from the moral stain of exploiting fellow human beings'

---

18. Cited in Beckert and Rockman, *Slavery's Capitalism*, 109.
19. Cited in Beckert and Rockman, *Slavery's Capitalism*, 111.
20. Cited in Beckert and Rockman, *Slavery's Capitalism*, 163.
21. Cited in Beckert and Rockman, *Slavery's Capitalism*, 167.
22. Cited in Beckert and Rockman, *Slavery's Capitalism*, 192.
23. Cited in Beckert and Rockman, *Slavery's Capitalism*, 278.

labor. This continues to be true today: none of our world today is free from the moral stain of exploiting fellow human beings' labor.

Siddarth Kara has documented modern slavery in the United States and around the world. While he has researched many forms of modern slavery, particularly sex trafficking, his research concerning agriculture in California and the fishing industry in Thailand show the far reach of modern slavery as it touches all of our lives. Kara acknowledges a variety of ways to define slavery and whether to use the language of *slavery* for today's forms of exploited labor. He offers the following definition: "*Slavery* is a system of dishonoring and degrading people through the violent coercion of their labor activity in conditions that dehumanize them."[24]

In California's Central Valley, Kara met over a thousand migrant workers and "documented the cases of 303 victims of labor trafficking."[25] Migrant workers migrate to the United States through regular or irregular channels. Kara explains, "Both regular and irregular migrant workers are recruited to travel to the United States for agricultural work by a labor recruiter called an *enganchadores* (literally, 'down payment'). Many irregular migrants make their way north across the border without formal recruitment by engaging a *coyote* on their own. In most of the cases of irregular migration I document, the coyotes facilitate the border crossing for migrants because they know the best routes for entry on any given day that will minimize the chances of interception by the U.S. border patrol."[26] Without official documents, migrants who have been recruited for agricultural work through irregular channels are most vulnerable to becoming victims of exploitation and modern slavery. "When labor trafficking occurs," Kara explains, "it is almost always exacted by the [farm labor contractor] or by the crew leaders."[27] The farm labor contractors or the crew leaders exact debts on the migrant workers for arranging the work that will take years to repay, if it is possible to repay at all.

In the summer of 2014, Kara met Enrique. Enrique was recruited from southern Mexico to work in the United States. In order to travel to the United States for work, he was required to pay a fee of $1,400. His family did not have the money, so his parents offered their land on loan to pay for the fee. After traveling by bus and on foot, Enrique was told that he must

---

24. Kara, *Modern Slavery*, 8.
25. Kara, *Modern Slavery*, 80.
26. Kara, *Modern Slavery*, 80.
27. Kara, *Modern Slavery*, 81.

pay an additional $700 to cross the border into the US. Since then, Enrique has worked on five different farms—avocado, orange, almond, lettuce, and walnut—without being paid what he was promised. However, he was told that if he complained then he would be reported and deported back to Mexico and his parents' land would be taken. After working for five years, he has no money. Enrique told Kara, "Please tell people there are thousands of Mexicans on these farms just like me. We share the same experience. We are forced to work like this because of poverty. I do not think the Americans realize where their food comes from. If they knew, they would not be happy."[28] Such stories may be repeated many times over.

Kara has investigated global supply chains in order to uncover exploitative labor practices, particularly in the fishing industry in Asia. "The presence of slavery in global seafood supply chains," Kara explains, "is a subset of a broader category of offenses called 'illegal, unreported, and unregulated' (IUU) fishing," and "more than half of global seafood exports from these regions are bound for the United States, the European Union, and Japan."[29]

Kara met Prak, a worker from Cambodia. Prak explained, "The recruiter said we can make good wages in Thailand. He said we will earn [$300] each month," and Prak continued, "When we arrived, he sold us to the ship captains ... The police at the docks said we had to go on the ships or they would arrest us for entering Thailand without documents."[30] Similar to migrant workers in California's Central Valley recruited from Mexico, Prak could either comply with being exploited or be deported. "I worked on the first ship for five months," and Prak said, "The guards treated us like animals. They shouted at us and beat us. We had to work all the time. ... If we complained, the guards tortured us. They chained us to the deck to burn in the sun. They threw men overboard to drown."[31] His harrowing experience is not from a distant past of chattel slavery. His story and many stories like his are happening now. People are reduced to units of exchange, recruited with deception, and exploited for labor.

The food on our tables depends on modern slavery, exploiting and dehumanizing vulnerable people. Many people "will be forced to work

---

28. Kara, *Modern Slavery*, 82–83.
29. Kara, *Modern Slavery*, 224.
30. Kara, *Modern Slavery*, 228.
31. Kara, *Modern Slavery*, 228–29.

until they are dead. That is the system."³² Moreover, "Price competition places powerful downward pressure on costs for producers," so "severe labor exploitation has become essential to the competitive profile of many Thai seafood exporters."³³ Consumers in the West desire more food and lower prices at the restaurant or grocery store, while the cost to human life remains hidden from the consumer's view. Kara draws into focus a contrast between slavery of the past and modern slavery.

> In the old world, slaves tended to be exploited for their lifetimes, whereas today individuals are exploited for much shorter periods of time. Due to the significant up-front costs of a slave centuries ago, and the relatively modest rate of capital recoupment, the slave owner tended to exploit his slave for a longer period of time. . . . [Today], most slaves, especially trafficked slaves, may be exploited for just a few months or at most a few years. . . . This shift is primarily due to the fact that the capital investment for acquiring a slave is much less today and can be recouped within just a few months. After that point, the slave owner is generating massive profits.³⁴

According to Kara's research, today enslaving people is a lower financial risk with a higher financial near-term gain than in the past. Though slavery has been made illegal in most of the world, "human life has become more expendable than ever before."³⁵ Kara explains, "The immensity and pervasiveness of slavery in the modern era is driven by the ability of exploiters to generate substantial profits at almost no real risk through the callous exploitation of a global subclass of humanity whose degradation is tacitly accepted by every participant in the economic system that consumes their suffering."³⁶ All of us who benefit from the global economy are complicit. What can a preacher possibly say while facing the enormity of such exploitation and suffering?

---

32. Kara, *Modern Slavery*, 230.
33. Kara, *Modern Slavery*, 241.
34. Kara, *Modern Slavery*, 25.
35. Kara, *Modern Slavery*, 25.
36. Kara, *Modern Slavery*, 254–55.

Feeding Capitalism's Hunger

LAND: TURNING PLACES INTO OBJECTS FOR CONSUMPTION, YESTERDAY AND TODAY

The exploitative consumption of people's suffering extends to exploitative treatment and plundering of land. Leonardo Boff has asserted, "If we want to see the brutal face of the capitalist and industrial system, we need only visit the Brazilian Amazon."[37] Boff has noted that the two greatest threats to the Amazon are clear-cutting and burning and that through all the centuries of colonization less than forty square miles were cleared. Since then, however, the destruction to the Amazon has been precipitous.[38] "Heavy industry," Boff explains, "has been set up in the Amazon in response to the demands of international capitalism."[39] Clear-cutting trees with a disregard for Indigenous communities has become more than routine. It has become violently orchestrated.

Boff describes a project developed by the American billionaire Daniel Ludwig. He conceived of a project that would involve nine million acres for producing wood pulp and exporting beef, rice, and soybeans.[40] The project was a reckless failure, as Boff says, "the result of ecological carelessness and ignorance."[41] Since they clear-cut the native trees and imported trees from Africa and Honduras for pulp wood, a fungus attacked and devastated the nonnative trees. In the end, Ludwig sold the land, but the greater loss was the loss of the native forest.[42] Though this was a project undertaken in the 1960s, it serves to illustrate the recklessness of focusing only on profit and ignoring the local ecosystem. Ignorance, however, is not the worst destructiveness in the Amazon. There are more sinister operations at work.

The treatment of Indigenous peoples in the Amazon by corporations is almost beyond belief. Boff states the obvious: "It is the Indigenous people who suffer most from the exploitation and internationalization of the wealth of the Amazon."[43] At the Serra Pelada mine, "forty thousand prospectors work out in the open," and the mercury flowing out of the mines and into the rivers kills fish, poisons fishermen, and ruins water for Indigenous

---

37. Boff, *Cry of the Earth, Cry of the Poor*, 86.
38. Boff, *Cry of the Earth, Cry of the Poor*, 91.
39. Boff, *Cry of the Earth, Cry of the Poor*, 96.
40. Boff, *Cry of the Earth, Cry of the Poor*, 91.
41. Boff, *Cry of the Earth, Cry of the Poor*, 92.
42. Boff, *Cry of the Earth, Cry of the Poor*, 92.
43. Boff, *Cry of the Earth, Cry of the Poor*, 99.

people.⁴⁴ At the far western end of the Amazon, tin mines were set up, and in order to get the Indigenous people out of the way, "the Arruda e Junqueira company ordered sacks of sugar dropped into a village during a ceremony. The Indians happily picked up the sugar, and then a plane flew over, dropping dynamite, and slaughtered them."⁴⁵ This was not an isolated incident. This was routine. The treatment of land and Indigenous people in the Amazon is morally reprehensible. It is as if land and Indigenous people are treated as morally irrelevant.⁴⁶

In addition to the Brazilian Amazon, few places on Earth vivify Boff's connection between the cry of the earth and the cry of the poor more than the Democratic Republic of the Congo. Siddharth Kara observes, "There is a frenzy taking place in the Democratic Republic of the Congo, a manic race to extract as much cobalt as quickly as possible. This rare silvery metal is an essential component to almost every lithium rechargeable battery made today."⁴⁷ Moreover, Kara explains, "No company wants to concede that the rechargeable batteries used to power smartphones, tablets, laptops, and electric vehicles contain cobalt mined by peasants and children in hazardous conditions."⁴⁸ Similar to the Brazilian Amazon, it is the land and local people who suffer most from the exploitation and internationalization of the wealth. The valuable resources are extracted and the local people are left poisoned and sick.⁴⁹

---

44. Boff, *Cry of the Earth, Cry of the Poor*, 98.

45. Boff, *Cry of the Earth, Cry of the Poor*, 99.

46. The treatment of land and Indigenous peoples by corporations in the Amazon is not unique. Rob Nixon recounts the Louisiana-based mining company Freeport McMoran, partnering with an Indonesian regime to pursue ethnocide as a means of development. Nixon comments, "Freeport's private security officers and the Indonesian military on occasion combined to shoot and kill unarmed Indigenous protestors." Freeport's chairman, James Moffet, said, "Freeport is thrusting a spear of development into the heart of West Papua." In response to the carnage and drawing together the lives of the land and the people, an Amungme leader said, "Freeport is digging out our mother's brain. That is why we are resisting." Nixon, *Slow Violence and the Environmentalism of the Poor*, 118.

47. Kara, *Cobalt Red*, 2.

48. Kara, *Cobalt Red*, 3.

49. Anna Lowenhaupt Tsing comments on the hidden dynamics of supply chains and inventory, as she writes, "Salvage translates violence and pollution into profit. As inventory moves increasingly under control, the requirements to control labor and raw materials recedes; supply chains make value from translating values produced in quite varied circumstances into capitalist inventory." *Mushroom at the End of the World*, 64.

Feeding Capitalism's Hunger

Kara documents extensively the supply chains that depend on "artisanal miners," who are men, women, and children. Kara notes, "The titanic companies that sell products containing Congolese cobalt are worth trillions, yet the people who dig their cobalt out of the ground eke out a base existence characterized by extreme poverty and immense suffering. They exist at the edge of human life in an environment that is treated like a toxic dumping ground by foreign mining companies. Millions of trees have been clear-cut, dozens of villages razed, rivers and air polluted, and arable land destroyed."[50] Kara has traveled and documented cases of exploitation and environmental catastrophe along the Copper Belt in the Democratic Republic of the Congo. "By virtue of geographic fluke, the Central African Copper Belt holds roughly half of the world's cobalt reserves at an estimated 3.5 million tons."[51] With renewable batteries in seemingly everything in sight in the West, the frenzy to extract as much cobalt out of the Copper Belt as possible is predictable, and the catastrophe is beyond reckoning.

Kara explored many towns, villages, mines throughout the Copper Belt. Around the city of Kolwezi, "the green is gone. Arable earth is extinct." As the home of around a fourth of cobalt in the world, Kara observes, "Kolwezi is the mangled face of progress in Africa."[52] Near the city of Kolwezi is Lake Malo, and at Lake Malo, Kara met Elodie, a fifteen-year-old girl, "scarcely more than bones and sinew." She carried her two-month-old son on her back. Elodie suffered from the late stages of HIV infection. Elodie had become an orphan as a result of cobalt mining. Her father had died when a tunnel collapsed. Her mother had died from an infection. After that, Elodie became a prostitute in order to survive. She slept in a hut with other orphaned children, and she was paid approximately 55 cents a day for her work digging cobalt at Lake Malo, which was not enough to pay for even the most basic necessities.[53] Later, when Kara went back to Lake Malo to reconnect with familiar people, he learned that Elodie and her baby were found dead under a thorn tree.[54] The stories of pain inflicted by exploitation of people and extraction of land are endless.

---

50. Kara, *Cobalt Red*, 5.
51. Kara, *Cobalt Red*, 24.
52. Kara, *Cobalt Red*, 158.
53. Kara, *Cobalt Red*, 178–79. After the first time I learned about Elodie's story, I prayed for her. Perhaps the prayer is pointless. It felt pointless, but I had to pray anyway.
54. Kara, *Cobalt Red*, 238.

Kara's research documenting numerous abuses of lands and local peoples is not simply an argument against clean renewable energy. Rather his research is a critique of governments, corporations, and economic systems that know of the abuses and do not rectify the problems with stronger protections for lands and fair compensation for workers. "Villages have been flattened. Forests have been razed. The earth has been gouged and gashed. Mines swallow all."[55]

When Apple reports being worth more than three trillion dollars, we should question how they are treating the land and how they are treating the local people and communities who are digging for the cobalt required for rechargeable batteries. How can it be that Apple can amass nearly incalculable wealth and many children dig with their hands for cobalt and earn less than a dollar per day? Should we be surprised that technological devices involving child labor leave us feeling depressed? In the face of rapid and exponential growth, we would do well to ask, "At what cost and at what cost to whom?" The lands and peoples who were once political colonies have been changed into economic colonies controlled by transnational corporations.[56]

In effect, like the Egyptian pharaoh in the Old Testament book of Exodus, Apple and similar corporations are expecting countless people to make bricks without straw, without basic necessities for work—all this while destroying lands and local ecosystems. It is as Kara has stated, "Our daily lives are powered by human and environmental catastrophe in the Congo."[57] What can a preacher, who is entangled in this system of exploitation and environmental catastrophe, possibly say?

LANDFILLS: TURNING PLACES INTO SITES FOR WASTE, YESTERDAY AND TODAY

Capitalism's hunger does not only exploit people and extract resources from land, capitalism's hunger also dumps toxic waste into poor communities, who often do not have the political or economic influence to prevent toxic waste from being dumped in or near their neighborhoods and schools. "Environmental justice" entered common parlance in the early 1980s.[58]

55. Kara, *Cobalt Red*, 157.
56. Berry, *Great Work*, 131–32.
57. Kara, *Cobalt Red*, 5.
58. Tsing, Deger, Saxena, and Zhou note, "Environmental justice must be inside, not

In 1982, a landfill designated for toxic waste was planned to be placed in Warren County, North Carolina, a predominantly African American community.[59] Dorceta E. Taylor has documented the history of hazardous waste facilities being "concentrated in minority and low-income communities."[60] The term "environmental racism" describes the processes by which minority communities face disproportionate environmental harms.[61] Taylor uses three questions to guide her research: "Why do minorities live adjacent to hazardous facilities or become exposed to environmental hazards? Why do they not move? And who or what keeps them from moving?"[62] Economically powerful corporations use every device at their disposal to cut costs and increase profits, even and often at the expense of minority and low-income communities.

Taylor outlines a study conducted in 1983 by Robert Bullard. In his study, Bullard found that toxic waste sites were not randomly or evenly spread across the city of Houston. Rather, "they were located in predominantly Black communities and near schools." He found that "four out of five of the city's incinerators were located in predominantly Black neighborhoods, while the fifth was found in a predominantly Hispanic neighborhood."[63] Other studies found similar results, that race was the "strongest predictor of the location of the commercial hazardous waste facilities."[64] These were studies focusing on corporations dumping hazardous waste in minoritized and low-income communities in cities in the United States. An additional element that Taylor suggests be used in future studies is an assessment of *"how hazardous"* the waste sites are and not only an assessment of how many waste sites are concentrated in and around minority and low-income communities.[65]

Native American tribal lands also have been the recipients of high concentrations of hazardous waste facilities. Taylor notes, "Native American reservations host many extractive industrial operations because tribal lands hold significant and strategic reserves of natural resources," and "not

---

an add-on to, Anthropocene studies." *Field Guide to the Patchy Anthropocene*, 38.

59. Taylor, *Toxic Communities*, 6, 13, 19.
60. Taylor, *Toxic Communities*, 1.
61. Taylor, *Toxic Communities*, 2.
62. Taylor, *Toxic Communities*, 3.
63. Taylor, *Toxic Communities*, 35.
64. Taylor, *Toxic Communities*, 36.
65. Taylor, *Toxic Communities*, 45.

only are reservations degraded by mining operations and contaminated by spills and dumping of hazardous wastes; reservations are heavily courted to become the temporary and permanent storage sites of high-level nuclear wastes from all over the country."[66] There are "326 reservations in the U.S.,"[67] and there are "317 reservations threatened by hazardous wastes."[68]

Valuable resources are extracted from Native American tribal lands and toxic wastes are dumped into the tribal lands. Taylor expresses the reality directly, as she states, "Corporations extract resources, which are converted into wealth, while [Natives] labor in unsafe conditions, live in poverty, and inherit perilous wastes."[69] The Skull Valley Goshute in Utah is but one example. It has been described as the "nation's highest concentration of hyper-hazardous and ultra-deadly materials" and a "national sacrifice zone."[70] Though living near toxic waste sites is dangerous for manifold reasons, Native Americans have expressed a desire to remain on the land because they represent important ties to their ancestral lands.[71]

Dina Gilio-Whitaker offers comments reinforcing the connection between colonization and the disposal of toxic waste on Native American lands. Gilio-Whitaker notes, "In the settler colonial context where the irreducible objective is attaining Native territory and resources, these bodies and lands are sacrificial and inevitably expendable because they are viewed and treated as worthless."[72] The treatment of Navajo Nation underscores her observation. Most of the United States' uranium deposits lie within the home of Navajo and Pueblo peoples. "With roughly half of the United States' recoverable uranium in New Mexico and half of that within the borders of Navajo Nation," Gilio-Whitaker explains, "The Kerr-McGee Company in 1948 set up mining operations with a ready-made workforce of under- or unemployed Southwest Indigenous peoples, predominantly Navajo. The business-friendly environment was ideal for the company, with no taxes, cheap labor, and no health, safety, or pollution regulations."[73] If maximizing profit margins is the driving force behind decision-making,

---

66. Taylor, *Toxic Communities*, 52.
67. Taylor, *Toxic Communities*, 50.
68. Taylor, *Toxic Communities*, 53.
69. Taylor, *Toxic Communities*, 54.
70. Taylor, *Toxic Communities*, 54.
71. Taylor, *Toxic Communities*, 67.
72. Gilio-Whitaker, *As Long as Grass Grows,* 64.
73. Gilio-Whitaker, *As Long as Grass Grows,* 65.

then exploitation of labor and land are the means of accomplishing those ends. The toxic waste, too, will threaten precisely the places where labor and land have been exploited. Gilio-Whitaker comments,

> Four months after the Three Mile Island nuclear plant meltdown in July 1979, on the Navajo reservation near Church Rock, New Mexico, an earthen dam disposal pool containing uranium mine waste burst, releasing a toxic stew of ninety-three million gallons of acidic, radioactive tailings and solid radioactive waste into the Rio Puerco River, poisoning the drinking and irrigation water of thousands of Navajo people as far as eighty miles downstream. The Rio Puerco catastrophe is generally thought of as the worst radiation spill in American history, even though it received nowhere near the attention of Three Mile Island.[74]

The exploitative practices of colonization are not a distant memory. Poor communities, who do not have the economic and political influence to defend themselves from corporations, are treated as sacrificial colonies within the United States. This is to say nothing of global efforts to dump more toxic waste from Western countries into African countries. The president of the World Bank, Lawrence Summers, suggested as much when he said, "I think the economic logic behind dumping a load of toxic waste in the lowest-wage country is impeccable."[75] The exploitative practices of colonization are ever present. What can a preacher, who does not share close proximity to toxic waste sites and who benefits from toxic waste being dumped elsewhere, possibly say?[76]

CONCLUSIONS: WE HAVE NORMALIZED DESECRATION

Though there is more to assess with regard to capitalism's violent hunger—including prison complexes, the militarization of national borders, and the oil industry[77]—I have sought to bring into view the link between the

---

74. Gilio-Whitaker, *As Long as Grass Grows*, 65.

75. As cited by Rob Nixon in *Slow Violence and the Environmentalism of the Poor*, 1.

76. Social strata may be mapped in part by one's distance from waste. DeLoughrey, *Allegories of the Anthropocene*, 127.

77. Rob Nixon observes, "For some eighty years, oil has been responsible for more of America's international entanglements and anxieties than any other industry. In 2009, the United States spent $188.5 billion on imported oil.... In the three decades from 1976 to 1997, the United States spent a further $7.3 trillion on securing its oil supply from the Middle East." Nixon, *Slow Violence and the Environmentalism of the Poor*, 72.

logic that exploits people and the logic that plunders the land by tracing historical realities of labor, land, and landfills. Larry Rasmussen succinctly observes, "The most polluting industries still go to the places where land, labor, and lives are cheap as they chase profits and the bottom line around the globe."[78]

The purpose here is not to be exhaustive but rather to draw attention to a preacher's historical positioning. Minimizing costs in production and keeping prices palatable for consumers drive much of the global economy, at the tragic expense of peoples and lands. All of us who benefit from the global economy are complicit in exploiting vulnerable peoples and lands. Western lifestyles depend on exploiting people, extracting resources from land, and dumping waste into vulnerable communities.

Meanwhile, I have been holding the question, "Are we preachers acclimated to empire's predatory economics destroying the Earth?" The moral absurdity and nihilism on which modern lifestyles in the West depends is beyond words. Consumer capitalism renders lands, the human, and the more-than-human as nothing more than commodities for profit or as obstacles to obtaining that profit. Men, women, children, and vast biodiverse communities are subjugated and ruined. By such short-sighted reductionism, in the West, people's relationship with the Earth is wounded and distorted. What happens to abused communities and the Earth, then, is seen as of little consequence, if we notice at all. In the past and present, we are entangled in vast systems of exploitation. This is the Anthropocene, an epoch in which a single species wreaks catastrophe on its own home.

The destructive practice of turning the land, the human, and the more-than-human into commodities for profit is morally reprehensible enough. However, so far, this consideration has not remarked on the sacred quality of place. Wendell Berry wrote,

> There are no unsacred places
> There are only sacred places
> And desecrated places.[79]

In April, 2016, a small group of women from the Standing Rock Sioux tribe set up camp to monitor the development of a pipeline construction that would connect Bakken Oil crude to an oil field tank in Illinois. Four years earlier, the tribal council had expressed opposition of all pipelines

---

78. Rasmussen, *Earth-Honoring Faith*, 208.
79. As cited by Carvalhaes in *Rituals at World's End*, 93.

going through sacred lands. They expressed this disapproval to Energy Transfer Partners. In September, 2016, when people sought to prevent digging on a sacred site, ETP brought in private security. They sprayed mace into people's eyes and unleashed a dog to attack the group of protesters.[80] Gilio-Whitaker notes, "The mayhem and viciousness of the attacks on American Indians was a chilling reminder of a history of brutality used against the Lakota Sioux by the U.S. military."[81] In the face of neocolonial violence, they were bearing witness that the land is sacred and should not be reduced to a commodity for profit.

We have lost our attunement to the sacred by turning peoples and places into commodities for profit. We have subsequently become often indifferent when peoples stand up to obstruct the alleged progress of capitalism for the hunger of cities' manifold desires. By feeding capitalism's hunger, we have disregarded love for neighbor[82] and honor for land.[83] We have normalized desecration.

PROMPTS FOR PREACHING PREPARATION— NOTICE WHERE YOU PREACH:

Learn the history and geography of the land on which you preach.

Use the history of the place to frame your preaching preparation.

Use the geography of the place to discern various forms of segregation and power dynamics in your community.

Notice where people live and work.

Note transit routes, whether those are freeways, bus stops, trolleys, or subways.

---

80. Gilio-Whitaker, *As Long as Grass Grows*, 2–4.
81. Gilio-Whitaker, *As Long as Grass Grows*, 4.
82. E.g., Mark 12:30–31.
83. E.g., Exodus 23:10–11; Leviticus 25:4.

Searching for Speech
"YOU WILL BE WITH ME"[84]
Luke 23:43
Good Friday

To the man crucified on the cross next to him, Jesus said, "You will be with me."

To the wrongfully accused on death row, Jesus says, "You will be with me."

To the estranged son who has become ensnared in a matrix of addiction, Jesus says, "You will be with me."

To those bearing wounds of post-traumatic stress disorder from wars declared long over, Jesus says, "You will be with me."

To those living in a cloud of grief and depression, Jesus says, "You will be with me."

To construction workers working the night shift, whose lives were cut short, Jesus says, "You will be with me."

To the unhoused man sleeping outside the church office, Jesus says, "You will be with me."

To students making decisions between spending money on books or food, Jesus says, "You will be with me."

To migrant families who have been separated for many long years, Jesus says, "You will be with me."

To those who are caught in a web of labor exploitation, Jesus says, "You will be with me."

To those struggling under the weight of insurmountable debt, Jesus says, "You will be with me."

To those navigating a labyrinth of under-employment, Jesus says, "You will be with me."

To those facing housing insecurity, who wonder whether they will have shelter next month or even next week, Jesus says, "You will be with me."

To those whose neighborhoods have been taken out from under them, Jesus says, "You will be with me."

---

84. I preached this sermon/poem on March 29, 2024, at Faith Presbyterian Church, San Diego.

To those whose neighborhoods have become dumping sites for toxic waste, Jesus says, "You will be with me."

To rural communities in this country and around the world, whose communities are used and disposed of by cities as mere resources, Jesus says, "You will be with me."

To visionaries creating art in the face of heart-wrenching ruins, Jesus says, "You will be with me."

To nonconformists planting gardens in the face of increasing militarism, Jesus says, "You will be with me."

To parents searching for their children amidst rubble, Jesus says, "You will be with me."

To the teenage mother with an infant on her back digging for cobalt in Congo, Jesus says, "You will be with me."

To children whose futures are uncertain, Jesus says, "You will be with me."

To Indigenous peoples whose homes are being decimated by transnational corporations, Jesus says, "You will be with me."

To birds choked by smog, Jesus says, "You will be with me."

To rivers poisoned by chemicals, Jesus says, "You will be with me."

To pollinators, bees and butterflies, killed by pesticides, Jesus says, "You will be with me."

To depleted topsoil and local farmers whose small farms have been closed by agribusiness, Jesus says, "You will be with me."

To the trees cut down to make a cross, Jesus says, "You will be with me."

To all the Earth groaning under the weight of insatiable extractivism, Jesus says, "You will be with me."

To each of us, to all of us, with the heartaches and wounds we carry every day, living and dying in the shadows of empire, Jesus says, "You will be with me."

"You will be with me."

"You will be with me."

"You will be with me."

Amen.

CHAPTER 2

Witnessing Worlds Disappear

"Mistreatment of one species
is mistreatment of all."[1]

SUZANNE SIMARD

"The forest is alive. It can only die if
the white people persist in destroying it.
The rivers will disappear underground, the soil
will crumble, the trees will shrivel up, and
the stones will crack in the heat."[2]

DAVI KOPENAWA

"Genocide seems all too often
to accompany ecocide."[3]

GEORGE TINKER

ONE OF MY FAVORITE trees to climb as a child was a dogwood tree with white flowers in my parents' front yard. I enjoyed feeling the variegated, gray and black bark under my fingertips. A fungal disease has since infected the dogwood trees in the region. Dogwood trees are no longer common and lining the roadways and fields. The dogwoods are disappearing. Only one remains on my parent's farm, and half of the branches are visibly

---

1. Simard, *Finding the Mother Tree*, 294.
2. Kopenawa, *Falling Sky*, after the maps section.
3. As cited by Rasmussen in *Earth Community Earth Ethics*, 85.

rotting. Soon dogwoods in the region will be only a fading memory from my childhood. When I attempt to comprehend what Western capitalistic civilization is doing to the Earth, I think of what that fungal disease has been doing to dogwood trees.[4]

While capitalism's insatiable hunger consumes lands and communities of the human and the more-than-human, the pillaging of lands and peoples does not have only short-term consequences, as painful as those are. The current extractivism is irreparably harming the Earth. E. O. Wilson stated the situation simply: "Life on this planet can stand no more plundering."[5] Whole worlds are disappearing.

There are many ways of bearing witness and speaking about the catastrophes encircling us. I have seen firsthand presenters drown an audience in statistics about climate change and ocean acidity. I believe that may be one of the least effective ways of communicating the realities of the Anthropocene. It is important to be familiar and set forth some of the basic facts of climate change that have wide-ranging implications for every species on the planet. As a preacher, however, I am particularly interested in learning how to speak about tragic events that are almost too large in time and space to grasp. Worlds may be disappearing in real-time, all around us, but how then do we talk about it? How do we speak effectively about environmental disasters driven, in part, by economic consumption? When the heart-wrenching events are counted in geologic time and on a global scale, what can possibly be said and what can be said that will resonate with listeners, whose lifespans are usually less than one hundred years but whose collective actions will bear the consequences for thousands of years or more? Rob Nixon describes the challenge of narrating what he calls "slow violence" that happens gradually, often out of sight, and is dispersed across time.[6] While our attention may be drawn to single, cataclysmic events, many environmental disasters are unfolding at a more elusive pace but with no less significant consequences.

---

4. Tsing comments, "Pathogenic fungi—fungi that kill—show us the dangers of the Anthropocene. Working together with human infrastructures, fungi have been responsible for more species extinctions than any other group of organisms," and she observes, "Pathogenic fungi have become collaborators in building a planetary Anthropocene without easy solutions." See Tsing, Deger, Saxena, and Zhou, *Field Guide to the Patchy Anthropocene*, 168, 190.

5. Wilson, *Creation*, 99.

6. Nixon, *Slow Violence and the Environmentalism of the Poor*, 2.

At the end of this chapter, I include prompts for preaching preparation, and I offer a sermon that introduces the concept of the Anthropocene and invites worshippers to bear witness to the life of trees in the Bible and in their lives. I offer a second sermon that introduces worshippers to the practice of bearing witness to the loss of biodiverse life. This chapter may prove most useful by reading the sermons at the end of the chapter first, reading the chapter, and then rereading the sermons again.

Gathering variegated narratives grounded in particular times and places may begin to draw our attention to ways in which "slow violence" touches upon lives in imbalanced ways around the world.[7] With the following four narratives, I am raising the question, "What are effective ways for preachers in the West to write and to speak about environmental catastrophe?"

QUESTIONS FOR REFLECTION IN PREPARATION FOR THIS CHAPTER—WITNESS AND EXTINCTION

When you walk outside, what are native trees on the patches of land you regularly cross?

Where do you witness trees being used as commodities in and for your daily life?

Can you begin to name and number the species who depend on the native trees on the patches of land you regularly cross?

What are declining species in your immediate area?

How might you begin to bear witness to declining species in your sermons?

What are the main water sources for your area and what is the health of the waterways and soils in your area?

---

7. This storied approached is inspired by Tsing, Deger, Saxena, and Zhou as they write, "Instead of regarding planetary climate change, assessed through modeling, as the only index of Anthropocene transformations, we consider how human infrastructures in particular times and places remake species, geologies, and, more generally, environments." *Field Guide to the Patchy Anthropocene*, 9.

THE DEATH OF RELATIONSHIP: WITNESSING THE RAVAGED RELATIONS WITHIN FORESTS

Suzanne Simard belongs to a family of loggers. Before she became a forest scientist, when she was twenty years old she began working for a logging company in western Canada. Her responsibility was to assess the health of saplings that had been planted to replace harvested trees. She remembers, "I tried to find any seedlings that were healthy, but to no avail. What was triggering the sickness? Without a correct diagnosis, the replacement seedlings would likely suffer too."[8] Nearby, in sharp contrast with the planted sapling spruce, she noticed that a sapling fir had begun to grow and appeared healthy with a strong root system. Why was the wild fir growing strong but the planted spruce suffering? This would be a question that would remain with her and guide her research for many years to come.

Later, she learned that various types of fungus form relationships—"a life-or-death liaison"—with plants. "Without entering into this partnership, neither the fungus nor the plant could survive." The fungus "gathered water and nutrients from the soil in exchange for sugars from the plant."[9] The fungus and the plant depended on each other in a mutual relationship. She began to wonder whether the planted sapling spruce, which was suffering, was unhealthy because it did not benefit from a mutual relationship with fungus as the wild and healthy fir did.

She did not stop at the discovery that trees and fungus can form a mutually beneficial relationship. She began to sense "that trees and plants could somehow perceive how close their neighbors were—and even *who* their neighbors were," and she continued,

> Pine seedlings between sprawling, nitrogen-fixing alders could spread their branches farther than if they hunkered under a thick cover of fireweed. Spruce germinants grew beautifully nestled right up to the wintergreens and plantains but kept a wide berth around the cow parsnips. Firs and cedars loved a moderated cover of birch but shrank when a dense cover of thimbleberry also grew overhead. Larch, on the other hand, needed a sparse neighborhood of paper birches for the best growth and the least mortality from root disease.

---

8. Simard, *Finding the Mother Tree*, 17.
9. Simard, *Finding the Mother Tree*, 59.

In Simard's estimation, the trees appeared to be aware, somehow, of who their neighbors were and with which neighbor they preferred to share close proximity. She wanted "to learn how trees sense and signal other plants, insects, and fungi."[10] In the process of her search for answers, she began asking an even more fundamental question: "Are forests structured mainly by competition, or is cooperation as or even more important?"[11] Many hold the perspective that the trees are competitive, so when planting a new crop of trees that will eventually be harvested, any and all competitor trees should be removed. However, Simard was beginning to question the wisdom of this practice.

Simard conducted an experiment with birch, fir, and cedar saplings. Her experiment involved determining whether the saplings were communicating. She explained, "My plan was to label paper birch with radioactive isotope carbon-14 so I could follow the photosynthate traveling to Douglas fir with the stable isotope carbon-13 to trace photosynthate move to paper birch. That way I could tell not only if carbon was passing from birch to fir but also distinguish if it was moving in the opposite direction, fir to birch."[12] She found that the birch and fir were communicating in the form of sending carbon to each other through their fungal partnerships in the soil.[13] Simard knew that cedar cannot form "fungal partnerships with the birch and fir."[14] The experiment only further confirmed that. She would later learn that "roots didn't thrive when they grew alone. The trees needed one another."[15]

As she continued to research, she learned that the trees were making decisions. "Over and over," she explained, "the experiments showed that carbon moved from a source to a sink tree—from a rich to a poor one—and that the trees had some control over where and how much carbon moved."[16] She began to conclude that she had "growing evidence that forests have intelligence."[17] Trees were all networked together with fungus, and the fungal partnerships could share carbon with other trees in the network when

---

10. Simard, *Finding the Mother Tree*, 100.
11. Simard, *Finding the Mother Tree*, 140.
12. Simard, *Finding the Mother Tree*, 147.
13. Simard, *Finding the Mother Tree*, 156.
14. Simard, *Finding the Mother Tree*, 148.
15. Simard, *Finding the Mother Tree*, 161.
16. Simard, *Finding the Mother Tree*, 185.
17. Simard, *Finding the Mother Tree*, 182.

there proved to be excess carbon.[18] "Ecosystems," she was realizing, "are similar to human societies—they're built on relationships."[19] Forests are fully alive like a human society, and she found that the older trees were taking care of the younger trees. "The old trees were the mothers of the forest."[20]

Simard's line of questioning began to go deeper in considering the intimacy and awareness trees share with each other. She wondered,

> If the mycorrhizal network is a facsimile of a neural network, the molecules moving among trees were like neurotransmitters. The signals between the trees could be as sharp as the electrochemical impulses between neurons, the brain chemistry that allows us to think and communicate. Is it possible that the trees are as perceptive of their neighbors as we are of our own thoughts and moods? Even more, are the social interactions between trees as influential on their shared relationships as that of two people engaged in conversation? Can trees discern as quickly as we can? Can they continually gauge, adjust, and regulate based on their signals and interaction, just as we do?[21]

Simard's research into the relationships between trees through their partnerships with fungus led her to experience forests as fully alive. "Solitude," she commented, "is rare in the forest."[22] Moreover, the trees meant more to Simard than fascinating objects for scientific experimentation. When she was grieving the death of her brother, she often went to the forest in search of "the promise of healing."[23] Not only were the trees connected with each other, she was finding connection with the trees. She expressed feelings of "compassion" for "the dying forest."[24] On another occasion, as she reflected on the magnitude of forests dying, she said, "There should be a special word for the type of mourning you know is to come."[25] These are not the sentiments of an emotionally detached person merely collecting objects for research. As she grew in her knowledge and experience of

---

18. Simard, *Finding the Mother Tree*, 186.
19. Simard, *Finding the Mother Tree*, 189.
20. Simard, *Finding the Mother Tree*, 228.
21. Simard, *Finding the Mother Tree*, 228–29.
22. Simard, *Finding the Mother Tree*, 222.
23. Simard, *Finding the Mother Tree*, 164.
24. Simard, *Finding the Mother Tree*, 255.
25. Simard, *Finding the Mother Tree*, 183.

witnessing families and neighborhoods of trees collaborating, she expressed the feelings of someone who shares a relationship. Later, she commented, "I was at home with these trees, my gentle friends, my confidants."[26] She had spent years learning as a scientist how the forest was communicating, and now she felt at home in the forest.

Clear-cutting old-growth, diverse forests for profitable, homogeneous crops is a short-sighted destruction of forests. Short-term profits result in long-term losses. E. O. Wilson commented, "The homogenization of Earth's ecosystems" is "painful and costly to our own species and will become more so."[27] Clear-cutting forests inflicts death on the relationships between the trees, plants, and fungus, to say nothing of the animals that rely on those relationships being healthy. The old growth, biodiverse forests are connected and take care of each other. When we destroy a forest and plant homogeneous crops, we are destroying whole networks of relationships of trees on which we all depend. We are killing families and neighborhoods of trees.

THE DEATH OF CHILDHOOD: WITNESSING THE RAPID DISAPPEARANCE OF SPECIES

When he was seven years old, with his mother suffering from mental illness and his father often absent, Michael McCarthy's family system was "being rent asunder."[28] But his love for the smallest creatures around him was only just about to begin. He remembers venturing into the backyard at his aunt and uncle's house and finding a "tall bush covered in jewels, jewels as big as my seven-year-old hand, jewels flashing dazzling color combinations: scarlet and black, maroon and yellow, pink and white, orange and turquoise."[29] They were not actually jewels, as he would discover. They were butterflies. He recalls, "I gazed up at them. I was mesmerized. My eyes caressed their colors like a hand stroking a kitten." And he remembers their indelible impression on him: "Wondrous? Electrifying, they were. Filling the space where my feelings should have been. And so, through this singular window, when I was a skinny kid in short pants, butterflies entered my soul."[30]

---

26. Simard, *Finding the Mother Tree*, 256.
27. Wilson, *Creation*, 54.
28. McCarthy, *Moth Snowstorm*, 8.
29. McCarthy, *Moth Snowstorm*, 5.
30. McCarthy, *Moth Snowstorm*, 5.

Witnessing Worlds Disappear

McCarthy has since spent his life as an environmental journalist, traveling the world documenting the life of the natural world. He traces his love for being outdoors back to when he was seven and encountered the bush with dazzling butterflies. Looking back to his childhood in Britain, he remembers,

> Suburban gardens were thronged with thrushes. Hares galumphed across every pasture. Mayflies hatched on springtime rivers in dazzling swarms. And larks filled the air and poppies filled the fields, and if the butterflies filled the summer days, the moths filled the summer nights, and sometimes the moths were in such numbers that they would pack a car's headlight beams like snowflakes in a blizzard, there would be a veritable snowstorm of moths, and at the end of your journey you would have to wash your windscreen, you would have to sponge away the astounding richness of life.[31]

He remembers the vibrancy of natural life from his childhood, but this vibrancy has begun to rapidly fade within his lifetime.

While his generation in Britain born after the World War II was the generation that has witnessed exponential growth, his is also the generation that "saw the shadow fall across the face of the earth."[32] He reflects,

> Already more than half the rainforests are gone, pesticide use has decimated wild flowers and the insect populations of farmland and rivers, the beds of seas are deeply degraded and most of the fish stocks are at danger levels, the acidity of the ocean is steadily rising, coral reefs are under multiple assault, 40 billion tons of climate-changing carbon are loading into the atmosphere every year and currently one fifth, and rising, of all vertebrates—mammals, birds, fish, reptiles, and amphibians—are threatened with extinction.[33]

All this may seem overwhelming and too much to grasp. McCarthy acknowledges that it is increasingly difficult to comprehend the losses and to know what they mean.[34] In his lifetime, Britain has "wiped out half its wildlife."[35]

---

31. McCarthy, *Moth Snowstorm*, 13.
32. McCarthy, *Moth Snowstorm*, 14.
33. McCarthy, *Moth Snowstorm*, 16.
34. McCarthy, *Moth Snowstorm*, 64.
35. McCarthy, *Moth Snowstorm*, 87.

To begin to picture the losses in a personal way, he recalls what he called the "snowstorm of moths" (see the quotation on the page just previous). On warm summer nights in the countryside, moths would appear to be numerous snowflakes crowding together in the headlight beams of a car speeding down the road. "Of all the myriad displays of abundance in the natural world in Britain," McCarthy commented, "the moth snowstorm was the most extraordinary, as it only became predictable in the age of the internal combustion engine. Yet now, after but a short century of existence, it has gone."[36] He has since spoken with people about their memories of the moth snowstorm and has asked them about the last time they saw such a multitude of moths crowding their car's headlight beams. They are invariably astonished that the phenomenon has since disappeared.[37]

McCarthy began writing anecdotally about the disappearance of the moth snowstorm in the year 2000, along with the decline of bees and insects in general. Several years later, agricultural researchers began releasing data about the decline of insects in Britain. His anecdotal experiences were being confirmed. He commented,

> Of the 337 species examined, two-thirds were declining: 80 species had declined by 70 per cent or more, and 20 of these had gone down by over 90 per cent. In southern Britain, three-quarters of moth species were tumbling in numbers; their total cumulative decline since 1968 was estimated at 44 per cent, while in urban areas, the losses were estimated at 50 per cent. The snowflakes which had made up the snowstorm were simply no longer there.[38]

Within McCarthy's lifetime, the world and beauty he knew as a child has been rapidly fading away and dying as a result of "the scale of the human enterprise."[39] As a consequence of the combination of habitat loss, invasive species (often carried accidently by human travel), pollution, exponential human population growth, and overharvesting, many species of insects and animals will continue to decrease rapidly and face extinction.[40] The world that so captivated McCarthy as a child is dying. Future generations will not experience the same vibrancy of the natural world in their childhood.

---

36. McCarthy, *Moth Snowstorm*, 102.
37. McCarthy, *Moth Snowstorm*, 102.
38. McCarthy, *Moth Snowstorm*, 105.
39. McCarthy, *Moth Snowstorm*, 14.
40. Wilson, *Creation*, 75.

THE DEATH OF HOME: WITNESSING VIOLENCE AGAINST INDIGENOUS PEOPLES

Davi Kopenawa desires to heal his people and protect the Earth as a Yanomami shaman, whose home is the Amazon rainforest. Kopenawa explains, "I was born in this forest and have always lived here."[41] He recounts his people's relationship with spirits and the forest. According to their tradition, *Omama* created them and taught them to name things.[42] The forest belongs to *Omama*. Kopenawa desired to be to become a shaman because he desired to gain wisdom and to heal his people.[43] An important part of a shaman's responsibility is protecting the "earth, as much for us and our children as for [white people] and [their children]."[44] It may be impossible to overstate the intimate connection Kopenawa and his people have with the forest. Kopenawa stresses, "Do not think the forest is empty."[45] The forest is alive and full of life, more than "just a great quantity of trees."[46] The forest is spiritual, rich with meaning and connection.

Kopenawa first encountered white people when they arrived unannounced, seeking to recruit people from his village to carry heavy loads through the forest.[47] Sadness and anger fill his words as he reflects on what happened after the white people arrived. "Many of us died after the arrival of these outsiders with their epidemic fumes and shotguns. We have been sad and known the anger of mourning too often."[48] He lost his father and mother as a result of illnesses that came with the arrival of white people.[49] In sum,

> Our minds get tangled with words about the gold prospectors who eat the forest's floor and foul our rivers, with words about the settlers and the cattle ranchers who burn its trees to feed their animals, with words about government that wants to open new

---

41. Kopenawa, *Falling Sky*, 21.
42. Kopenawa, *Falling Sky*, 22.
43. Kopenawa, *Falling Sky*, 113.
44. Kopenawa, *Falling Sky*, 151.
45. Kopenawa, *Falling Sky*, 62.
46. Kopenawa, *Falling Sky*, 65.
47. Kopenawa, *Falling Sky*, 174.
48. Kopenawa, *Falling Sky*, 26.
49. Kopenawa, *Falling Sky*, 169, 198.

roads here and tear minerals out of the ground. We fear malaria, flu, and tuberculosis.[50]

For Kopenawa and his people, white people's arrival has been nothing less than an invasion and desecration of the forest and their community. They arrived with the intention, Kopenawa says, "to take possession."[51]

The pattern would often repeat itself. The white people would arrive asking for help and offering gifts. Then, they would seek to possess everything—the minerals in the ground, the trees, the land, the women and children, and the mind of the Yanonami people. The combination of Western developers and missionaries has decimated the forest and the Yanomami people.

On one particular occasion, a group of white men came to Kopenawa's village. They were led by a man named Oswaldo. He desired one of the young girls. He began giving gifts to the young girl's parents, but the elders of the village did not wish for the young girl to be taken by Oswaldo. In the beginning, Oswaldo was friendly. When he was refused, he became angry and left without saying anything. He returned with a metal box. He buried it in the ground and lit an explosive. The metal box exploded and spread what appeared to be a lethal smoke. Many people became sick and died, including the young girl Oswaldo had desired.[52] The arrival of the white people meant death in every direction and for everyone.

In the beginning of the white people's arrival, they came on the rivers, but it did not remain that way. Kopenawa remembers,

> When I was a child, the white people came up the rivers in big canoes and made a great number of our elders perish. Then they came back by airplane and helicopter. Once again their epidemic fumes made many more people die. Now they have decided to open one of their roads all the way into the heart of the forest. I knew that their diseases would probably devour those of us who had survived until then.[53]

The development of roadways only accelerated the devastation of the rainforest and the people who call the rainforest home. Moreover, the development of roadways through the rainforest was without the local people's

---

50. Kopenawa, *Falling Sky*, 160.
51. Kopenawa, *Falling Sky*, 177.
52. Kopenawa, *Falling Sky*, 179–81.
53. Kopenawa, *Falling Sky*, 234.

knowledge. Local people were not consulted. Developers did not ask, "Can we clear this path on your land? What do you think? Won't it frighten you?"[54]

Kopenawa was perplexed by white people's behavior. He wondered why they spent so much money breaking apart the forest when they have people back in their land living on the streets. Kopenawa reflected, "I contemplated the wounded forest and, deep inside me thought, 'Why did their machines put so much effort into tearing out all the trees and this soil?'" and he continued, "'Why waste their money like this when in their cities many of their children sleep on the ground like dogs?'"[55] Kopenawa perceived a contradiction: the white people arrive to steal and destroy someone else's home, while they had not cared for people in their own home. In the centers of their cities, the houses are beautiful, but on the edges, people have "no food and their clothes are dirty and torn."[56] The white people have a problem. They are sick. Kopenawa reflected, "I constantly thought of the forest, which had become as sick as the humans."[57]

Kopenawa desires to defend the forest and his people, his home. "We refuse to let our land be destroyed," he says, and "we do not want our forest to die, covered in wounds and the white people's waste. We are angry when they burn the trees, tear up its floor, and soil its rivers. We are angry when our women, our children, and our elders constantly die from epidemic fumes. We are not white people's enemies. But we do not want them to come work in our forest because they cannot return the value of what they destroy."[58] To white people and those who extract the resources from the rainforest, he says, "You often claim to love what you call nature. Then do not settle for making speeches, truly defend it. . . . All its inhabitants already speak to us with fear of disappearing."[59] The losses Kopenawa and his people have suffered are heartbreaking and beyond measure.

Kopenawa recognizes that white people are beginning to think ecologically, and he hopes they will begin to see the environment as one interconnected whole, not merely individual parts. Kopenawa is searching for ways of speaking that people can receive and says, "I am always searching

54. Kopenawa, *Falling Sky*, 235.
55. Kopenawa, *Falling Sky*, 252.
56. Kopenawa, *Falling Sky*, 349.
57. Kopenawa, *Falling Sky*, 274–75.
58. Kopenawa, *Falling Sky*, 280.
59. Kopenawa, *Falling Sky*, 323.

for other words; words they do not know yet. I want them to be surprised and to open their ears."⁶⁰ There is such a wide chasm between Yanomami ways of being and Western ways of being. It can be difficult to begin to grasp the depth and intimacy Yanomami people have with the forest. The forest is sacred, filled with countless relations. Kopenawa says, "The white people, with their mind set on merchandise, do not want to hear us. They continue to mistreat the earth everywhere they go, even under the cities they live in," and "this is why today I search for powerful words to say how much all this angers me."⁶¹ As a shaman, Kopenawa is a defender of the forest and a healer of his people.

THE DEATH OF DEATH: PRACTICING RESURRECTION WITH TREES AND LOCAL COMMUNITIES

"A great river always begins somewhere. Often it starts as a tiny spring bubbling up from a crack in the soil, just like the little stream on my family's land in Ihithe,"⁶² Wangari Maathai observed. The great river of her life sprang up from the small village of Ihithe in the central highlands of Kenya. She was the third of six children and the first girl after two sons. Her parents were peasant farmers of the Kikuyu community.⁶³ As a scientist and activist and first woman to receive a doctorate in East and Central Africa,⁶⁴ Wangari Maathai founded the Green Belt Movement, an environmental initiative to heal local communities and the land by planting trees. The seeds for what would later evolve into the Green Belt Movement were planted in her imagination as she witnessed the devastation of the land and the direct negative impact devastation of land had on rural communities, and especially on women.

Maathai traced the historical unfolding of devastation, as she observed, "When European missionaries came to the central highlands at the end of the nineteenth century, they taught the local people that God did not dwell on Mount Kenya, but rather in heaven, a place above the clouds," and she continued, "Within two generations, they lost respect for their own beliefs and traditions. The missionaries were followed by traders and

60. Kopenawa, *Falling Sky*, 353.
61. Kopenawa, *Falling Sky*, 354.
62. Maathai, *Unbowed*, 119.
63. Maathai, *Unbowed*, 3.
64. Maathai, *Unbowed*, 113.

administrators who introduced new methods of exploiting our rich natural resources: logging, clear-cutting native forests, establishing plantations of imported trees, hunting wildlife, and undertaking expansive commercial agriculture."[65] She draws a historical line connecting theology that belittled the significance of the land to exploitative practices that devastated local environments for short-term gains. "Hallowed landscapes," she explained, "lost their sacredness and were exploited."[66] She acknowledged, "I was born as an old world was passing away."[67] She recalled that in the 1940s the British colonial government was burning down native forests and planting commercial plantations of non-native trees.[68] When local peoples in Kenya revolted, the British responded with extreme severity, creating "detention camps, effectively concentration camps" with "more than one hundred thousand Africans, mostly Kikuyu," dying in "concentration camps and emergency villages."[69] The violence of colonization devastated the people, place, and culture of Kenya.

As she began to notice the problems of cultural and environmental catastrophe, Maathai perceived the problems to be intersectional, involving the lived experiences of gender, ethnicity, poverty, and land. Deforestation in service of coffee and tea crops was making an observable impact on soil erosion and silt in rivers. The people directly affected by the negative consequences of deforestation were women in rural communities, whose lives depended on what the land could produce. Deforestation made it more difficult for rural women to gather firewood and to cook nutritious food for their families.[70] She explained, "Women were feeding their families processed foods. . . . Cooking these foods consumed less energy . . . and this made them attractive and practical, because available firewood for cooking was limited due to deforestation." She desired not only to address the symptoms of environmental catastrophe but also the causes. She recalled, "It just came to me: 'Why not plant trees?' The trees would provide a supply of wood that would enable the women to cook nutritious foods," and she

---

65. Maathai, *Unbowed*, 5–6, 8. She also notes that most of the missionaries in her area were Scottish Presbyterians and Italian Catholics. The role of Presbyterians in connection with European colonization is of particular interest to me because my family shares a Presbyterian heritage on both sides of my family.

66. Maathai, *Unbowed*, 6.

67. Maathai, *Unbowed*, 7.

68. Maathai, *Unbowed*, 38.

69. Maathai, *Unbowed*, 66, 68.

70. Maathai, *Unbowed*, 121, 123.

continued, "They would heal the land by bringing back birds and small animals and regenerate the vitality of the earth."[71] By encouraging and coordinating efforts for women in rural areas to plant trees, not only did she seek to heal the physical landscape, she sought to lift up and empower women.

On June 5, 1977, in celebration of World Environment Day, Maathai participated in a processional and tree-planting ceremony. Seven trees in honor of seven people from different ethnic groups were planted. "These seven trees," Maathai explained, "formed the first 'green belt.'"[72] Though there were many challenges and setbacks for the Green Belt Movement, eventually, as local farmers, schools, and churches joined the effort, the seeds of the Green Belt Movement were planted throughout Kenya.

Wangari Maathai dedicated her life to healing communities and the land by planting trees. This dedication took many forms, and much of the time it put her at odds with her own government, which preferred the incentives of immediate profits over the long-term benefits of empowering local communities to form healthy relationships with the land. She advocated for the empowerment of women in rural areas, protested the devastation of parks and forests, and promoted the rights of political dissidents. She explained, "For me, the destruction of the Karura Forest, like the malnourished women in the 1970's, the *Times* complex in Uhuru Park, and the political prisoners detained without trial, were problems that needed to be solved, and the authorities were stopping me from finding a solution."[73] In her words, through it all, "We remained unbowed."[74]

Maathai perceived the roots of the problem of environmental catastrophe to begin with European colonization of Africa that devastated local cultures, landscapes, and political imagination. She often used planting trees as an actual response to the devastations of colonial projects and as a symbol of what could be possible. "How did we register our protest?" She asked. "Our answer was to plant trees."[75] In 2004 she was awarded the Nobel Peace Prize. She reflected, "Trees are living symbols of peace and hope. A tree has roots in the soil yet it reaches to the sky. It tells us that in order to aspire we need to be grounded, and that no matter how high

---

71. Maathai, *Unbowed*, 125.
72. Maathai, *Unbowed*, 132.
73. Maathai, *Unbowed*, 272.
74. Maathai, *Unbowed*, 222.
75. Maathai, *Unbowed*, 273.

we go it is from our roots that we draw sustenance."[76] In the midst of a death-dealing history, a history of European colonization that devastated her people, culture, and land, Maathai rose up like a tree with roots planted in the soil and branches reaching for the sky. Could planting trees be the death of death?

CONCLUSIONS: MOVING BEYOND "STEWARDSHIP OF CREATION"

Our way of life in the West sows death across the face of the Earth. With Suzanne Simard, we perceive that the biodiverse world around us and of which we are a part is alive and communicating, and when we destroy the biodiverse world for profit, we are destroying vast networks of relationships that we are still only beginning to learn about. With Michael McCarthy, we witness the rapidity with which we are destroying the biodiverse world, and if we continue on the same course we are on, the vibrancy of the biodiverse world he remembers from his own childhood will be hardly more than a fading memory. With Davi Kopenawa, we hear the voice of one who loves the rainforest and whose home is being decimated in the name of progress and profit. With Wangari Maathai, we recognize hard-won resilience and hope in the face of death-dealing colonization and environmental catastrophe. Their social locations could hardly be more different: a Canadian biologist, a British journalist, a Yanomami shaman, and a Kenyan activist. More than their social locations, their cosmologies are also widely divergent—as a Western Christian I struggled with writing notes as I read Davi Kopenawa without rapidly losing and inadvertently erasing his cosmology with my Western Christian cosmology, at best touching upon but never fully grasping[77] his ways of being in the world.[78] In each case and in vary-

---

76. Maathai, *Unbowed*, 293.

77. Mayra Rivera describes "transcendence in the flesh of others whom we touch, but may never fully grasp." *Touch of Transcendence*, 2.

78. Linda Tuhiwai Smith observes, "The arguments of different Indigenous peoples based on spiritual relationships to the universe, to the landscape and to stones, rocks, insects and other things, seen and unseen, have been difficult arguments for Western systems of knowledge to deal with or accept. These arguments give partial indication of the different world views and alternative ways of coming to know, and of being, which still endure in the Indigenous world. Concepts of spirituality which Christianity attempt to destroy, then to appropriate, and then to claim, are critical sites of resistance for Indigenous peoples." *Decolonizing Methodologies*, 84.

ing ways, Simard, McCarthy, Kopenawa, and Maathai witnessed what and whom they loved under existential threat from the voracious hungers of capitalism. They were not speaking only from planetary facts; they were speaking from broken hearts grounded in particular times and places.[79] Moreover, their narratives can help us "see ourselves as others would see us."[80] Stepping beyond our immediate social location and looking back at our social location and its many environmental complicities can be a useful homiletical move.

As a preacher, part of what I find most remarkable is not only that we are witnessing worlds disappear around us in real time but that our way of life in the West actively contributes to the destruction of our own backyards as well as people and places we will likely never see. Moreover, the manifold devastations of ecosystems are not only short-term exploitations that need to be rectified—such as appropriately compensating people for labor. Rather, the manifold devastations of species and ecosystems are irreparable in the long term. We need witnesses to ritualize and to articulate the irreparable catastrophes encircling us every day. We need witnesses who will speak to the minds and hearts of people in our churches. We need witnesses to shake us awake from our stupor. In this sense, pastors and spiritual leaders would do well to listen and to draw wisdom from people of many different traditions, including Indigenous people whose homes are being destroyed for Western hunger.

In 1990 a Thai Buddhist monk, Pharkru Pitak, decided to ordain trees in response to the deforestation and resultant soil erosion impoverishing the land. Pitak wrapped "the big old trees—the ones most desired by the timber companies—in saffron robes, ritually investing them with the status of Buddhist monks."[81] To cut down a tree would be tantamount to killing a Buddhist monk. Pitak put a sign on the trees that read, "To destroy the forest is to destroy life." He drew upon the symbolic and moral world of his community in order to convey the sacredness of trees and the forest on which all of their lives depended. Larry Rasmussen observes, "The sacred values conveyed by the saffron robe had trumped the monetary value of timber for the market. The choice was not an easy one—jobs, already in

---

79. These four narratives, however, remain largely anthropocentric. What if instead of foresters, journalists, shamans, and activists as the protagonists in our stories, we shift our stories to center trees, moths, rivers, and mountains? How would such a shift change our attention, values, and relationship with the lands we occupy?

80. Spivak, *Critique of Postcolonial Reason*, xii–xiii.

81. Rasmussen, *Earth-Honoring Faith*, 30.

short supply, were at stake—but it was real."[82] Pitak witnessed and protected their biodiverse community against the short-sighted hunger of capitalism.

In 2003, in response to a decision in South Korea to build a twenty-mile-long sea wall that would choke the life out of tidal flats for industry and agriculture, two Korean Buddhist monks and two Korean Christian ministers desired to express their sorrow with the creatures that would die as a result of an estuary's destruction. They led a *samboilbae*. The word means three steps and a bow. From Saemangeum to Seoul, the two Korean Buddhist monks and two Korean Christian ministers took three steps and then bowed to the ground. They repeated this process over and over. They completed the *samboilbae* in difficult weather conditions over the course of sixty-five days. They drew wide-ranging attention to the devastating impact of industry on biodiverse life, and when they finally arrived in Seoul, they were welcomed by more than 8,000 people.[83]

We are witnessing worlds disappear in real time. We may speak about God's good creation and humans as stewards of creation. Yet, such an approach does not take seriously the historical positioning of a speaker and listener in relation to colonization and capitalism. When we participate in a society whose primary guide and animating force is profit, we must do more than affirm God's intention and our role in biblical language. We have a responsibility to be attuned and to articulate our particular historical positioning without pretending that we continue to live in the same realities as the biblical communities 2,000 years ago. If we continue to preach as if our world and our historical realities remain the same as tribal desert kingdoms 2,500 years ago, then we will continue to passively and actively participate in destroying relationships in the biodiverse world, the world we knew as children, and the homes of the human and the more than human. We will be responsible for muting the biblical message of stewardship. Worse, we will be imposters, pretending stewardship is somehow compatible with widespread environmental devastation.

PROMPTS FOR PREACHING PREPARATION— NOTICE HUMAN IMPACT

As you learn the history and geography of the place in which you preach, learn the human impact on your biodiverse community.

82. Rasmussen, *Earth-Honoring Faith*, 30–31
83. McCarthy, *Moth Snowstorm*, 67–68, 79.

Searching for Speech

Note the impact of roadways on migration patterns of diverse species.

Learn local and regional decline of species and how biodiverse life depends on those species.

Note interconnections between species.

Learn Indigenous peoples' stories of the land.

Learn histories of colonization in your area from Indigenous peoples' perspectives.

"PAYING ATTENTION, FACING LIMITS"[84]

Genesis 3:1–24

Nearly seven years ago, shortly after Ezra was born, I went to my doctor for a routine visit. My doctor and I talked about a variety of areas of life, including family and children. At one point in the conversation, my doctor began to lecture me about having a really large family with a lot of children, and he said, "be fruitful and multiply, isn't that the *command* in Genesis?" Many things were rattling around in my mind as he began lecturing me, but because I wasn't sure that I wanted to end the relationship—a good doctor can be hard to find—I chose to say, "As a human species, I think we have more than fulfilled that mandate." He then pivoted to arguing for preserving what he believed to be American culture, and I then pivoted to deciding that perhaps I should find a different doctor. Several months later, he retired. I am not merely picking on my former doctor. Upon further reflection, I have realized that what my doctor was doing in that moment was what many of us probably do with the Bible.

We read and apply the Bible in our lives as if nothing has happened since the Bible was written, and we suppose that we somehow occupy the same space and understanding of the world as the biblical writers. Of course, that is not quite right. A lot has happened since then. In our case, with "be fruitful and multiply," in the past fifty years, the human population has doubled, and in the past hundred years the human population has multiplied by nearly eight times over. For some perspective, when John Calvin wrote his now famous *Institutes of Christian Religion*, there were estimated to be less than half a billion people in the world. Today, we will soon cross

---

84. I preached this sermon on May 7, 2023, at Faith Presbyterian Church, San Diego.

the threshold of eight billion people. We are now living in an era that some scientists call, the Anthropocene—from the word *anthropo*, meaning human. In other words, we live in an era in which the impact of humans in many ways determines the future of the earth.

All this to say, a lot has changed in our world, and I do not want us to pretend like nothing has happened in the world or in our lives since these stories in Genesis were first shared. So, as we read the Bible together, I want us to consider, "What wisdom and inspiration do these stories offer us today, for the time in history in which God has called us?"

Today, as we reflect on this ancient Hebrew poetic narrative, in Genesis chapter three, I want to invite us to do something simple. Notice the trees. I want us to notice the role of trees in this story and in our lives today.

The Bible begins and ends with trees, beginning in the book of Genesis and ending in the book of Revelation. The Bible begins and ends with trees. According to Genesis, in the garden of Eden, there was abundance. And there were two special trees, one the tree of life, and the other, the tree of the knowledge of good and evil. Adam and Eve were invited to enjoy everything in the garden, except for the tree of the knowledge of good and evil. While there was abundance, there was also a limit. God instructed them not to eat from the tree of the knowledge of good and evil.

The story in today's passage in Genesis is almost so familiar that we may have trouble seeing anything fresh about it. We can easily roll this story around in our minds. The clever serpent entices Eve to eat the fruit from the forbidden tree. Eve gives the fruit to Adam. After Adam eats the fruit, Adam and Eve's eyes are opened. They see that they are naked, exposed, vulnerable. They sow fig leaves together for clothes, to cover themselves. When God searches for them, they hide among the trees. This story feels as old as time.

Since the fifth-century theologian Augustine of Hippo, this story has been often portrayed as Adam and Eve's fall from innocence, and they represent humanity's fall from innocence. Following that line of thinking, humanity has inherited both their guilt and their sin-prone nature.[85]

Of course, in conversation, we may speculate about who really was responsible, who really was the guilty one. We may wonder, "How could Adam be so gullible? How could Eve be so easily enticed? And who made the serpent so clever, anyway?"

---

85. Hick, *Evil and the Love of God*, 207.

This ancient Hebrew poetic narrative has captured the imaginations and curiosity of generations. But, I want to invite us to read this story not only as an ancient story, but as a story that continues to repeat itself, a story that repeats itself in our lives today.

In the garden of Eden, trees nourish human life. In Jewish writings about the tree of life, they imagine that the tree of life was so large it would take 500 years to climb. It was larger than life and a source for life.[86]

In the garden of Eden, trees also set a limit to human life. That is especially important for today's chapter in Genesis. The tree of the knowledge of good and evil was a limit that Adam and Eve were not to cross. To cross this limit would be to trample the harmony of the garden. It is also no small poetic detail or accident that after Adam and Eve feel the desire to hide from God—where do they hide?—they hide among the trees. Genesis chapter three is a story about crossing and trampling the limits required for the harmony and abundance of the garden.

Today, trees have been called the lungs of the earth. We literally depend on trees to breathe. "Tree leaves pull in carbon dioxide and water and use the energy of the sun to convert this into chemical compounds such as sugars that feed the tree. As a by-product of that chemical reaction, oxygen is released by the tree."[87] We depend on trees to breathe. And this is especially important as humans have grown in number exponentially in recent years. We literally depend on trees for our life.

The biologist Janine Benyus has observed, "Nature is a measure. After 3.8 billion years of evolution, nature has learned: what works. What is appropriate. What lasts."[88] If we pay close attention, our relationship with trees can offer us a clue for how we are doing as caretakers of God's creation. Are we crossing the limits of trees?

In his Pulitzer Prize-winning novel *The Overstory,* Richard Powers describes environmental activists strapping themselves to trees and camping out in the tops of trees to prevent the destruction of nearly thousand-year-old Redwoods and to slow down deforestation. Camping out in the tops of trees may not be on your weekend to-do list. However, in the novel, I found fascinating the circuitous paths that these people in the novel traveled in their relationship with trees and their eventual care for forests—everyone

---

86. Sleeth, "Power of a Green God," 21.
87. Stancil, "Power of One Tree."
88. Carvalhaes, *Green People and Earth Communities,* 123.

from a Vietnam veteran to a college senior with one semester left to graduate. Each of them found their way to trees.[89]

And this is not only the stuff of fiction. There is a small Presbyterian church in San Francisco with a beautiful sanctuary. Their sanctuary was built with Redwoods. A year ago, as part of a service project for Lent, they raised money to plant the same number of Redwoods that were used to build their sanctuary. When I learned about that, I thought that was an absolutely lovely gesture. It may not solve all the issues with deforestation, but they are paying attention to the time and place they are in. They paying attention to their relationship with trees, and they are taking practical steps.

Our relationship with trees can offer us a clue for how we are doing as caretakers of God's creation. Genesis chapter three is not merely a story that describes something that happened one day long ago. It is, I believe, a story that repeats itself over and over again in our lives, as we continue to plunder and cross the limits of creation. Genesis chapter three is a parable for our time.

There are more than a few Christians taking their relationship with trees seriously, and this is not simply a new idea. So, do not go home today thinking that all this focus on trees and care for the Earth is something that I came up with last night because I was looking for a sermon topic.

In Ethiopia, there are church forests, and they are more than a metaphor. Ethiopian Orthodox faith teaches that for a church to be a church, it should resemble the garden of Eden. In one particular region in Ethiopia that has been devastated by agriculture businesses, there is a church of the forest, completely enveloped by trees, and it is a mutual relationship. The church keeps the forest, and the forest keeps the church. The church has been protecting the forest for centuries. Members of the forest church explain, "If the church loses the forest, the church will lose itself." And they continue, "There is a problem always, a misperception that these forests will stay forever. We don't have any other backup. To safeguard the Ethiopian biodiversity is only the church forests. If we lose that, then that's all. . . . So, if you really care, we have to respect the trees. We have to learn to live with forests."[90]

And, this is not only Ethiopian Orthodox teaching. The Protestant Reformer Martin Luther was asked what he would do if he knew the world

---

89. Powers, *Overstory*.
90. Carvalhaes, *Rituals at World's End*, 109–10.

was ending tomorrow. Luther famously answered, "I would plant a tree." He would plant a tree as an act of defiant hope.[91]

Matthew Sleeth, an emergency room doctor, recalls when his perspective and his life began to change. His experience has spoken to my heart and ignited my imagination. Matthew remembers on one February break, his family left the gray winter of northern New England and headed to an island off the coast of Florida for vacation. On the second day, their two children wore themselves out playing in the surf and building sand castles.

After their children went to bed early, his wife, Nancy, turned to Matthew and asked, "What is the biggest problem facing the world?" Matthew thought of many things—war, terrorism, poverty, disease, starvation, and at the root of everything, selfishness. Finally, Matthew said, "The world is dying."

He was not only thinking about abstract ideas. Many changes had taken place in his life and were readily apparent to anyone with eyes to see. The last of the majestic chestnut trees near his childhood home are now extinct. There are no chestnut trees on Chestnut Lane, no elms on Elm Street, no caribou in Caribou, Maine, and no buffalo in Buffalo, New York.

Nancy asked, "What will you do about it?" At that time, Matthew had no answer.

When they went home, Matthew's journey began. They began calculating all the energy they used and the trash and pollution they made. In other words, they began seeking to measure their environmental footprint. They decided to downsize in all areas of their lives to reduce their footprint. After joining a church to a have a spiritual grounding for their environmental concerns, Matthew began talking about some of his concerns and a friend at the church asked, "You're not one of those tree huggers, are you?" After going home and realizing that no one in their new church family seemed remotely concerned about the environment, Matthew continued to reflect. He found that a study of Scripture and thousands of years of writings by theologians and saints reveals a cohesive vision regarding believers' responsibility to care for the Earth.

Finally, Matthew reflected, "Like Adam in Genesis, we are expected to return the service of the garden with service of our own. This is a reciprocal service. This mutual service defines the relationship between garden and gardener, between the biosphere and its safeguarding stewards," us.[92]

91. Brueggemann, "Trees."
92. Sleeth, "Power of a Green God," 21.

Paying attention to trees, facing our limits, and recognizing our responsibility are nothing new. Many people have been attentive for a long time. Genesis chapter three is a parable for our time.

As people of faith, we have a responsibility to accept our limits as creatures and to care for the place God has called us.

Today and tomorrow and the next day.

Slow down.

Take a look around.

Pay attention.

Notice the trees in your life.

"REVERENCE FOR LIFE"[93]

Romans 8:18–25

The times in which we live may cause us to easily lose hope. And yet, throughout the course of my life, I have been awed by the human spirit, human resilience in the face of calamity. Whenever there is a crisis, neighbors show up for each other. Even people from different regions or countries or cultures show up to assist each other. Over and over again, we witness this reality. People inspire each other with their actions to hold onto hope. This is in part what the apostle Paul was doing in writing his letter to house churches in Rome in the first century. He wanted to inspire them with hope.

In his letter to house churches in Rome, Paul knew writing to Rome was a complicated affair. He knew that only a few short years earlier many Jews were expelled from Rome, and they returned only to find that gentiles—that is, everyone else—had taken over the church.[94] Jewish and gentile house churches then found themselves working out their faith in community but conflicting with each other. That is a significant part of the occasion of this letter: forming community across significant cultural differences.

The Letter to the Romans is a tightly woven story with layer upon layer of allusions to other stories. Paul doesn't miss an opportunity to build upon Israel's stories from the ancient past. He does this because he wants

---

93. I preached this sermon on April 21, 2024, at Faith Presbyterian Church, San Diego. On February 16, 1919, Albert Schweitzer preached a sermon entitled "Reverence for Life," in which he said, "Reverence for the infinity of life means removal of the alienation, restoration of empathy, compassion, and sympathy." *Reverence for Life,* 108.

94. Smith and Kim, *Toward Decentering the New Testament,* 206.

to show that God has kept and now fulfills promises. That is the gospel, the good news. God has been faithful in the past and will continue to be faithful. In the earliest chapters of Romans, Paul recalls creation and fall from the Old Testament book of Genesis. Paul describes God's goodness and creative power. Paul underlines the fact that humanity has been hard-hearted and has *not* recognized God. Creation and fall.[95] Paul also recalls covenant and law from Abraham to Moses. Paul recalls covenant and law as a way of showing that the covenant people have become part of the problem, not the solution.[96] In their failure to live up to the law, Israel is on a similar footing as other peoples of the world. Covenant and law.[97]

Today, in chapter eight of Romans, we find a spectacular panorama of the creation story and the exodus story coming together. So, Paul speaks of creation waiting eagerly for freedom and redemption. That is the creation story and the exodus story coming together. Paul writes to house churches in Rome about nothing less than their hope. And that is hope not only for themselves, but for all of creation. The gospel is good news for all of creation, not only for humanity. The hope about which Paul speaks should instill in us a reverence for life, and that is a reverence for all of life.

Now, yes, I will admit, I chose this text from Romans, in part, because tomorrow is Earth Day. And yet, I also wanted to start our reading of Romans at the climax, the crown jewel of the letter, as it has sometimes has been called, because I want us to begin by recognizing that the gospel of God, God's good news for the world, is good news for the whole creation, the entire cosmos.

We can take a brief look around and empirically confirm what Paul writes so poetically; that is, everything is falling apart. Or, as Paul says, creation has been subject to futility, enslaved to decay, groaning in labor pain.

Paul's audience in the first century could well have thought about how what Paul was saying was true. Paul's audience could have seen how the Roman empire's ambitions had led to the erosion of the natural environment throughout the Mediterranean world, leaving ruined cities, depleted fields, deforested mountains, and polluted streams. Paul's audience could easily imagine what he was describing.[98]

---

95. Romans 1:18–4:25.
96. Romans 2:17–29.
97. The above follows N. T. Wright, *Paul*, 29–30.
98. Jewett, *Romans*, 513.

Witnessing Worlds Disappear

The time in which we live is also a time of suffering for all of creation. We can take a brief look around and confirm that, indeed, things are falling apart. The journalist Michael McCarthy has noted, "Already more than half the rainforests are gone, pesticide use has decimated wild flowers and the insect populations of farmland and rivers, the beds of seas are deeply degraded and most of the fish stocks are at danger levels, the acidity of the ocean is steadily rising, coral reefs are under multiple assault, 40 billion tons of climate-changing carbon are loading into the atmosphere every year and currently one fifth, and rising, of all vertebrates—mammals, birds, fish, reptiles, and amphibians—are threatened with extinction." In his own home in Great Britain, McCarthy has stated, "Of the 337 species [of insects] examined, two-thirds were declining: 80 species had declined by 70 per cent or more, and 20 of these had gone down by over 90 per cent."[99]

Yes, things are falling apart. And yet, Paul exclaims, "For in hope we were saved. Now hope that is seen is not hope, for who hopes for what one already sees?" He was writing nearly 2,000 years ago. Could he have imagined the world we are facing and living in today? Well, no, I do not think so. And yet, Paul's message of persistent hope remains vital for us today.

Paul holds onto hope for the whole creation, the entire cosmos, because of who he knows God to be in Christ. God in Christ desires the healing and wholeness, the salvation of all of creation. And that message remains true for us today. Paul's message should instill hope in our hearts for ourselves and for all of creation. And this hope calls us into a reverence for all of life.

Paul describes the whole of creation eagerly waiting for the children of God to be revealed; as the children of God are revealed and through their transformed living, they will set creation free from its enslavement to futility and decay. To use more modern language, the children of God will restore the ecological system that has been put out of balance from wrongdoing. So, the creation, Paul says, eagerly longs for these transformed children of God who will take responsibility.[100] The task before us is enormous. What can we possibly do?

The American Christian ethicist Reinhold Niebuhr said, "Nothing that is worth doing can be achieved in our lifetime; therefore, we must be saved by hope. Nothing which is true or beautiful or good makes complete sense in any immediate context of history; therefore, we must be saved by

---

99. McCarthy, *Moth Snowstorm*, 16.
100. Jewett, *Romans*, 512.

faith. Nothing we do, however virtuous, can be accomplished alone; therefore, we are saved by love. No virtuous act is quite as virtuous from the standpoint of our friend or foes as it is from our standpoint. Therefore, we must be saved by the final form of love which is forgiveness."[101]

Nothing we do in this life will be complete or perfect. As we practice a reverence for life in perhaps small ways each day, we may feel like we are not solving big issues at all. But that does not mean we should give up and lose hope and resign ourselves to what seems inevitable. We need each other, and we need to encourage each other in hope. Each of us will at various times in our lives needs someone else to encourage and inspire us in hope.

In 1990 a Thai Buddhist monk, Pharkru Pitak, decided to do something far out of the ordinary. He faced the enormity of deforestation by corporations in Thailand. What could he, a mere monk, possibly do? This Thai Buddhist monk, Pharkru Pitak, decided to ordain trees in response to the deforestation and resultant soil erosion impoverishing the land. Pitak wrapped "the big old trees—the ones most desired by the timber companies—in saffron robes, ritually investing them with the status of Buddhist monks."[102] Harming a tree would then be equivalent to harming a Buddhist monk. Pitak put a sign on the trees that read, "To destroy the forest is to destroy life." He drew upon the symbolic and moral world of his community in order to convey the sacredness of trees and the forest on which all of their lives depended. The American Christian ethicist Larry Rasmussen observed, "The sacred values conveyed by the saffron robe had [surpassed] the monetary value of timber for the market. The choice was not an easy one—jobs, already in short supply, were at stake—but it was real."[103]

Ordaining trees may seem pretty far out of the ordinary to us. After all, it took centuries for us Presbyterians to ordain women. Pharkru Pitak, no doubt, knew that ordaining trees would seem strange to many people, but he also likely knew that if he did so, he could inspire his community to practice a reverence for life in the place in which they were living, in a time in which many people may have begun to lose hope that they could do anything to stop or at least slow down deforestation.

In 2003, in response to a decision in South Korea to build a twenty-mile-long sea wall that would choke the life out of tidal flats for industry

---

101. As cited by Rasmussen, *Earth-Honoring Faith*, 338.

102. Rasmussen, *Earth-Honoring Faith*, 30.

103. Rasmussen, *Earth-Honoring Faith*, 30–31.

and agriculture, two Korean Buddhist monks and two Korean Christian ministers desired to express their sorrow with the creatures that would die as a result of an estuary's destruction. These two Korean Buddhist monks and two Korean Christian ministers decided to lead a pilgrimage. From where the wall was to be built[104] all the way to Seoul, the capital city (about 200 miles), these two Korean Buddhist monks and two Korean Christian ministers practiced a ritual (*samboilbae*).[105] They took three steps and then bowed to the ground.

At this moment in the sermon, I stepped out from the pulpit to the middle of the stage and proceeded by demonstrating the ritual gesture of three steps and a bow. Then I returned to the pulpit and finished the sermon.

They repeated this process over and over for 200 miles. They completed this pilgrimage with this ritual in difficult weather conditions over the course of sixty-five days.

As they continued their pilgrimage with this ritual, they drew wide-ranging attention to the devastating impact of industry on biodiverse life, and when they finally arrived in Seoul, they were welcomed by more than 8,000 people.[106] These two Korean Buddhist monks and two Korean Christian ministers in South Korea desired to inspire their community to practice reverence for life in the place in which they were living, in a time in which many people may have begun to suppose that environmental destruction was inevitable or necessary. They did not want their people to give up and lose hope and resign themselves to what seemed inevitable. They were practicing reverence for life and inspiring their people to hold onto hope.

When the apostle Paul wrote to house churches in Rome, he desired to instill hope in their hearts. He desired to inspire them to persevere faithfully in the times in which they lived. They belonged to God, and this world belongs to God. We can continue to hold onto hope for their lives and for the life of the world with transformed living.

As Christians, as the church today, this is a vital part of our vocation. In a world of despair, and in the face of environmental calamity, we are people of enduring, tenacious hope.

---

104. The city of Saemangeum.
105. The word means three steps and a bow.
106. McCarthy, *Moth Snowstorm*, 67–68, 79.

CHAPTER 3

Where to Begin? With Whom?

> "The trees are so old that
> my lifetime compared to theirs
> is just a birdsong."[1]
>
> ROBIN WALL KIMMERER

> "What to a settler's eye seemed savage,
> untouched wilderness usually turns out
> to be landscapes actively managed by Indigenous
> populations for thousands of years through controlled
> burning, weeding, coppicing, fertilizing and
> pruning, terracing estuarine plots to extend
> the habitat of particular wild flora, building clam gardens
> in intertidal zones to enhance the reproduction of shellfish,
> and creating weirs to catch salmon, bass and sturgeon."[2]
>
> DAVID GRAEBER AND DAVID WENGROW

> "Do not be conformed to this age,
> but be transformed by the renewing of the mind,
> so that you may discern what is the will of God,
> what is good and acceptable and perfect."[3]
>
> ROMANS 12:2

---

1. Kimmerer, *Braiding Sweetgrass*, 206.
2. Graeber and Wengrow, *Dawn of Everything*, 150.
3. NRSVUE.

Where to Begin? With Whom?

Through a window in the church's sanctuary, I peered across the courtyard and saw a barefooted, middle-aged man wearing beekeeper's equipment walking briskly across the grassy courtyard. The church campus resides across the street from the main entrance of San Diego State University, so I have become acquainted with many unique people passing through the church's courtyard. This person looked like a man with resolve, eyes clear and piercing, with something pressing on his mind.

I walked outside and over to him and said, "Do you love bees?" Those were the first words that stumbled out of my mouth to a complete stranger.

And, he said, "Yes, I love bees. I know God's purpose for my life, and it feels good." Those were the first words that flowed from his mouth. They seemed to come easily and naturally to him.

I said, "Right, let me show you the beehive."

He said, "Great, let's take a look."

I was smiling all the way, as we walked to the countless bees swarming all over the place. That week, we had encountered multitudes of bees in the church's preschool playground. As it would turn out, a whole hive of bees had been growing right under our noses, creating honey for more than a week without us knowing. We called a professional beekeeper, who creates bee sanctuaries, to relocate the bees to a more appropriate location. When the beekeeper arrived and I led him to the bees, he deftly placed the hive in a cardboard box and left it there for three hours. When we returned, all the bees had found their way into the cardboard box with the queen in the hive. I could hardly believe relocating the bees could be so simple.

Earlier in the week, when several preschool teachers found bees swarming in the church's preschool playground, a conversation ensued about using pesticides. Together, we faced a decision. We could kill all the bees today so the preschool children could return to the playground soon, or we could relocate the bees the following evening, which was the next available time for the beekeeper.

When faced with a decision whether to use pesticides or schedule a beekeeper to relocate the hive, we decided to wait a day and schedule the beekeeper to relocate the bees. It was not the most efficient or least expensive decision, but it was the better decision. The decision was better for the bees, and the decision shifted something within us. We felt the joy of protecting life, and we felt a renewed commitment to caring for everyone in our community, including pollinators. The following month, reports indicated that millions of bees were dying in San Diego County.[4] Several months after that, a colleague in San Diego contacted me requesting advice on bee relocation. Our horizons of awareness and care were expanding and were in turn expanding the horizons of awareness of those around us.

Christy Lefteri describes a family's relationship with bees in her novel *The Beekeeper of Aleppo*. The beekeeper, Nuri, says,

> The bees were an ideal society, a small paradise among chaos. The worker bees traveled far and wide to find food, preferring to go to the furthest fields. They collected nectar from lemon blossoms and clover, black nigella seeds and aniseed, eucalyptus, cotton, thorn, and heather. I cared for the bees, nurtured them, monitored the hives for infestation or poor health. Sometimes I would build new hives, divide the colonies, or raise queen bees—I'd take larvae from another colony and watch as the nurse bees fed them with royal jelly.[5]

Later, Nuri's cousin, Mustafa, says, "The bees are family to us."[6] On his journey fleeing war, Nuri finds a bee without wings and decides to hold it in the palm of his hand. It is a tender moment of care and shows a form of kinship between Nuri and the bee. The description of his capacity to show delicate attention for another species has kindled my imagination with possibility. Just as the beekeeper I met in the church courtyard expressed his love for bees, Nuri demonstrates a gentle awareness for the bee's well-being. "When we extend our view of kinship beyond our anthropocentric view," Sherri Mitchell Weh'na Ha'mu Kwasset observes, "a whole new world of knowledge becomes available to us."[7]

At the end of this chapter, I include prompts for preaching preparation, and I offer a sermon that integrates a beekeeper's understanding of vocation into the church's spiritual life. Following that, I offer a second sermon that I preached for the San Diego Presbytery's Leadership Day. In the second sermon, I invite participants to inventory the losses they have experienced, the unarticulated laments that they carry in their hearts, and the grief they hold in their bodies. These invitations create space for deeper reflection on the tender places within their own lives in connection with the tender places in the Earth's life. As we grow in our tenderness with the

---

4. Lunetta, "What Killed 3 Million Honey Bees in North County?"
5. Lefteri, *Beekeeper of Aleppo*, 10.
6. Lefteri, *Beekeeper of Aleppo*, 18.
7. Mitchell, "Indigenous Prophecy and Mother Earth," 24.

Earth, we may begin to feel and to see the wounds of the Earth, and as we begin to feel and to see the wounds of the Earth, we may begin experiencing shifts in conversation partners and homiletical authorities as we grow in our preaching vocation with the Earth.

The traditions with whom preachers and congregations listen can transgress scientific disciplines, cultures, religions, politics, histories, geographies, and nation-state borders. We may begin by asking a series of generative questions that will vary depending on one's local context and social location. When we respond to the questions below, we may begin to discern who our guides will be to help us transform our vision of "here." These questions, moreover, may give rise to the creation of further place-specific questions. These questions are only a beginning. These questions will likely generate more questions. This chapter may prove most useful by reading the sermons at the end of the chapter first, reading the chapter, and then rereading the sermons again.

Eurocentric ways of being have promoted narrow views of progress and profit nearly everywhere in the world. Western colonization has rendered the material life of a given place as potential commodities for profit. Such a narrow view of the world has prized human advancement without considering the cost to biodiverse ecosystems to which we belong. The result has been nothing short of catastrophic, with destruction to ecosystems everywhere. Eurocentric theology will provide a similarly limited view of possibility in relation with the Earth. The material life of a given place bears little consideration for the substance of theology and homiletics. This raises fundamental questions for preachers. With regard to a given place, "Where do we go for our source material for preaching? And who will be our homiletical authorities?" But, before addressing those questions directly, we may ask, "What does the Anthropocene look like 'here'?" While tracing logics of extractivism and patterns of extinction are crucial for perceiving the broad-scale impact humans are having on the planet, preachers can start with where we are. Preachers begin "here." If we preachers begin "here," then we can ask, "Who loves this place, now and in the past?" They will guide us. They will lead us into the places and perspectives from which our sermons will arise.

Searching for Speech

QUESTIONS FOR REFLECTION IN PREPARATION FOR THIS CHAPTER—SEARCHING FOR HOMILETICAL GUIDES

Where are signs of life in the ruins of the Anthropocene?

Who is listening and speaking on behalf of trees, rivers, marshes, pollinators, and mountains?

Who is planting seeds of biodiverse possibility in your local community?

Who is advocating for policies to protect local biodiverse ecosystems?

Whose homes are being decimated by extractivist corporations and environmental catastrophe?

Who is defying, in small and large ways, the extractivist practices of transnational corporations and the exponential growth of militarization?

WHERE TO BEGIN? TAKING AN INVENTORY OF "HERE"

Preachers begin by peering out the window and taking a step outside. We begin where we are. We begin "here." While biblical texts may animate a preacher's theological imagination, preachers do not preach looking down at the text. Preachers preach by looking up to the world. The Irish poet David Whyte has described reality itself as a conversation, particularly in his poem "Everything Is Waiting For You." Whyte invites us to awaken to the "intimacy of [our] surroundings"—everything from the "soap dish" to "the window latch" to "the stairs" are actors with us in the drama of life.[8] Preachers, then, look up to the world and share a conversation with the reality of "here." We begin with the people and place in which we live, eat, sleep, meet, study, serve, celebrate, grieve, laugh, and encounter all the ingredients of daily life. We begin with the ground on which we walk, the wind in our face, the sun on the back of our neck, the rain in our hair, and the ocean waves crashing against our chest. Each and every fiber of "here" contributes to forming our identities as preachers in community. Preachers always preach from "here." That is an inescapable fact. It may be obvious, but it requires prayerful and critical attention.

Preachers may begin "here." Yet, beginning "here" may itself prove elusive. "For now we see only a reflection, as in a mirror," as the apostle Paul

---

8. Whyte, *Everything is Waiting for You*, 6.

wrote in his Letter to the Corinthians.⁹ We see "here" through inherited cultures, histories, and technologies that form our perception. As a child growing up in rural South Carolina, the fact that the routine planting and harvesting of trees for pulpwood felt as normal to me as the four seasons is a significant hint of industrial capitalism shaping my imagination and vision. It did not occur to me as a child that methodically pillaging the landscape for profits was peculiar and harmful to local biodiverse communities encircling me. Inherited cultures, histories, and technologies animated my vision of "here."

Diana Butler Bass recalls a time when she went on a personal retreat. She remembers she was sitting in the center of a labyrinth at Mount Calvary, a monastery in Santa Barbara. The labyrinth was painted on a concrete patio in a garden, behind an old building that now serves as a retreat house. Bass reflects, "At the edge of the labyrinth were native plants and flowers, including a bright purplish bush called woolly blue curls, where a hummingbird—oblivious to my presence—feeds."¹⁰ Her desire to reconnect with the life of the Earth is laudable, yet when she observes a hummingbird, she assumes the hummingbird was "oblivious" to her presence. With her industrialized Western vision, she perceived the hummingbird as an object and not a fully active subject participating and aware in the local community.¹¹ Bass's vision of the hummingbird as informed by inherited cultures, histories, and technologies becomes all the more obvious when juxtaposed with Francis of Assisi's vision of a cricket outside his monastery window. On one occasion, Francis observed a cricket in a tree, and as he peered out the window, he said, "My sister cricket, come to me. Sing, my sister cricket, and praise your Creator with a joyful song."¹² Francis perceived himself as one creature among many. While Bass and Francis may reside in historically and culturally different geographies, their juxtaposition accentuates elements of the elusive task of seeing "here." Who and what constitutes "here"? With what inherited cultures, histories, and technologies do we perceive "here"?

---

9. 1 Corinthians 13:12.

10. Bass, *Grounded*, 1.

11. A young boy told Laurens van der Post, "One is never alone in the forest. One is never unobserved." *A Far Off Place*, 79, as cited by Berry, *Great Work*, 179.

12. Boff, *Cry of the Earth, Cry of the Poor*, 211.

Edward Said's analysis of Europe's invention of the "Orient"[13] may provide further insight for how inherited cultures, histories, and technologies can diminish and obscure one's vision of the world. Said observed, "In many ways my study of Orientalism has been an attempt to inventory the traces upon me, the Oriental subject, of the culture whose domination has been so powerful a factor in the life of all Orientals."[14] The violent historical traces of colonialism and industrialism have impressed themselves on the West's vision of the "Orient" and on the subject of the West's vision. Said felt this vision particularly pressing itself upon him as an Arab Palestinian living in America. "The web of racism," he reflected, "cultural stereotypes, political imperialism, dehumanizing ideology holding in the Arab or the Muslim is very strong indeed, and it is the web which every Palestinian has come to feel as his uniquely punishing destiny."[15] Following the historical and political contours of Europe's invention of the "Orient," Said noted, "Once we begin to think of Orientalism as a kind of Western projection onto and will to govern over the Orient, we will encounter few surprises."[16] When the West's culture, history, and technologies become the aesthetic filter for one's field of vision, whole constellations of life become artificially transmuted into mere objects. Said explained, "A white middle-class Westerner believes it is his human prerogative not only to manage the nonwhite world but also to own it, just because by definition 'it' is not quite as human as 'we' are."[17] Seen through the West's filtered vision, anyone and anything not white and Western are rendered objects. This diminishes and obscures one's vision of oneself and of the world. Edward Said's analysis of Europe's vision of the "Orient" should offer a warning and an invitation to practice epistemic humility and self-critical assessment. Our vision of a place and a people will often be severely limited and obscured. Like Europe's dehumanizing and objectifying vision of the "Orient," a vision of "here" will be inescapably animated and shaped by inherited cultures, histories, and technologies, many of which have wounded the Earth.

In order to unravel our assumptions about and projections onto "here," we can inventory the traces upon ourselves, observing the inherited cultures, histories, and technologies that animate and shape our vision.

13. Said, *Orientalism*, 1.
14. Said, *Orientalism*, 25.
15. Said, *Orientalism*, 27.
16. Said, *Orientalism*, 95.
17. Said, *Orientalism*, 108.

Cláudio Carvalhaes inventories the traces of colonialism in his own life, as he notes, "Friends, this is not an inventory of celebrations but an inventory of tragedies, war zones, abandonment, pain, death, and destitution."[18] To inventory the traces of colonialism on ourselves requires facing the horrors of history, culture, and technology that shape our lives with the life of the Earth. Carvalhaes explains, "The notion of *inventory* I employ is an activity to revisit our past and name what has brought us this far."[19] Taking an inventory of culture, history, technology, and all the realities that have brought us to the present "here" is an activity preachers and congregations can do together. Carvalhaes often uses the language of "lingering"[20] to invite a slower-paced inventory. Preachers and congregations can ask themselves together, "What are the hidden histories and assumptions that animate our vision of 'here'?" Taking a slow-paced inventory that "lingers" can open a broader and deeper field of vision for seeing "here," for seeing the wounds and the gifts of "here," and for creating a more inclusive understanding of the subjects of "here."

One cultural assumption to identify and abandon is Western industrialism's reduction of everyone and everything's value to a matter of utility.[21] When everyone and everything is reduced to a mere object of utility, then everyone and everything is discarded when their utility comes to an end—a plastic bottle is discarded when its contents have been consumed or a person is discarded when their ability to produce has been exhausted. This diminished vision of life has wreaked havoc across the face of the Earth, rendering oceans and mountains as objects for consumption. We need a vision of life that values everyone and everything as worthy of moral regard. Preachers and congregations can ask themselves together, "In what ways are we reducing the manifold forms of life encircling us to mere objects of utility?" Moreover, in view of colonialism's historical and ever-present wounds, preachers and congregations may ask themselves together, "In what ways are we perpetuating a theology of conquest in our vision of 'here'?"[22]

---

18. Carvalhaes, *How Do We Become Green People and Earth Communities?*, 27.
19. Carvalhaes, *How Do We Become Green People and Earth Communities?*, 28.
20. Carvalhaes, *How Do We Become Green People and Earth Communities?*, 27–29.
21. Berry asserted, "'Use' as our primary relationship with the planet must be abandoned." *Great Work*, xi.
22. Mendoza and Zahariah observe, "Our contemporary mainstream ecotheologies tend to develop their own ecotheological visions and ethics without dismantling this creation theology of conquest and displacement." *Decolonizing Ecotheology*, 3.

We need a transformation of vision. When we inventory the inherited cultures, histories, and technologies that animate our vision, this inventory will involve a transformation not only in what we see but also in how we see. Like colonial settlers failing to see the ways in which Indigenous peoples managed land,[23] we will need to unlearn our ways of seeing in order to appreciate the fullness of "here." The Earth is alive and communicating all around us, all the time. With our colonial settler's cultures, histories, and technologies, we have a lot of unlearning and relearning to do in order to value the fullness of relationships encircling us "here." If we begin to perceive ourselves as but one subject among multiplicities of other subjects, the Earth will come alive to our senses, and we will find ourselves intimately connected within the life of the Earth.

Upolu Luma Vaai reflects on the Oceania vision of oneself in relationship with the life of the Earth, saying, "There is no disconnection of earth and people. I am a walking land! A moving earth! . . . For Oceanic communities, anything that is body-related, that they belong to, that is part of them, they will protect and care for it."[24] This vision runs in stark relief to a vision that reduces everyone and everything to an object of utility. Though trading a Western vision for an Indigenous vision may not be possible any more than turning back time to a romanticized period of history in which people lived in harmony with "nature," a relational vision of oneself as within the Earth opens up fields of possibility with diverse cultures and contemporary science. In his exploration of microbes, Ed Yong reflects, "Every individual is more like an archipelago—a *chain* of islands. Each of our body parts has its own microbial fauna, just as the various Galapagos islands have their own special tortoises and finches."[25] We contain multiplicities of life, and we are intimately connected with multiplicities of life encircling us in ways our eyes fail to perceive and our inherited cultures, histories, and technologies diminish and obscure. An Oceania vision of oneself as connected with the life of the Earth may seem too far for Western eyes to shift, but an Oceania vision values what contemporary science confirms: a relational vision of the world.[26]

---

23. Graeber and Wengrow, *Dawn of Everything*, 150.

24. As cited by Mendoza and Zahariah, *Decolonizing Ecotheology*, 4.

25. Yong, *I Contain Multitudes*, 17.

26. We should be careful, however, to resist forms of what Renato Rosaldo describes as "imperialist nostalgia" in which the same Western people, cultures, and institutions responsible for destruction "long for the very forms of life they intentionally altered or destroyed." As cited by DeLoughrey, *Allegories of the Anthropocene*, 188.

Where to Begin? With Whom?

Merlin Sheldrake raises a question that is worth preachers and congregations lingering with awhile: "Are we able to stand back, look at the system, and let the polyphonic swarms of plants and fungi and bacteria that make our homes and our worlds be themselves, and quite *unlike* anything else? What would that do to our minds?"[27] Can preachers and congregations linger long enough to let the polyphonic voices of "here" touch and transform how we see ourselves and the life of the Earth?

Thomas Berry recalled what he described as a "magic moment" on an early afternoon one late May. When he was eleven years old, his family moved to a new house with a hill that sloped down to a creek. He crossed the creek and encountered a meadow covered with white lilies rising above thick grass. He recalled, "It was not only the lilies. It was the singing of the crickets and the woodlands in the distance and the clouds in the clear sky," and he continued, "Perhaps it was not simply this moment that made such a deep impression on me. Perhaps it was a sensitivity that was developed throughout my childhood . . . Whenever I think about my basic attitude and the whole trend of my mind and the causes to which I have given efforts, I seem to come back to this moment and the impact it has had on my feeling for what is real and worthwhile in life." Berry concluded, "Whatever opposes this meadow or negates it is not good."[28] His ethics, theology, economics, and general priorities arose from the meadow. The meadow taught him how to see himself and the world around him.

In our search for "here," we will find that we have finally begun to see "here" when we take an inventory of our inherited cultures, histories, and technologies. We will find that we have finally begun to see "here" when we identify and feel the colonial wounds of "here." We will find that we have finally begun to see "here" when we relinquish cultural assumptions that reduce the life of the Earth to objects of utility. We will find that we have finally begun to see "here" when we perceive ourselves as intimately joined to "here" in ways that our eyes fail to see and that our hearts have only just begun to understand and imagine. When we begin to perceive ourselves as intimately joined to all the constellations of life that constitute "here," we will find ourselves wanting to learn from the life of bees, age-old trees, hummingbirds, and meadows, not as objects of "nature" but as subjects with whom we are entangled in the vast and beautiful web of Earth's life.

---

27. Sheldrake, *Entangled Life*, 174.
28. Berry, *Great Work*, 12–13.

Perhaps, we will want to sing with crickets, and we may eagerly ask, "Who loves this place, now and in the past?"

WITH WHOM?
WORKING WITH MULTIPLICITIES OF WISDOMS

Preachers begin "here" with their spiritual community. But, then, who constitutes a preacher's spiritual community? Is it limited only to official members of a church or regular participants in the spiritual community? Who constitutes a preacher's spiritual community that will expand, deepen, challenge, and enhance both the preacher's and the spiritual community's vision of "here"? Is it limited to a particular region, culture, language, religion, politics, race, class, tradition, sexual orientation, or gender? Is it limited to the human realm, even while affirming and celebrating multiculturalism? Who constitutes a preacher's spiritual community that will show both the preacher and the spiritual community how to love "here"?

Our vision of "here" will require an ongoing process of unlearning and learning afresh. Our vision of "here" can be guided by natives and genealogies of natives who have loved this place, now and in the past. If the West's cultures, histories, and technologies have often been bent on death-dealing extraction, then we will need to search beyond the confines of the West's cultures, histories, and technologies. Moreover, Eurocentric theology has been of little help, prizing white Western human life, while sacrificing everyone and everything else. Kwok Pui-Lan argues for "transnational and multicultural origins and genealogies."[29] We can relinquish the primacy of a single tradition.[30] We can hold epistemic humility with a posture and a desire to love the places in which we live. Furthermore, moving beyond simple cultural appropriation and instead being transformed by multiplicities of cultural origins and genealogies, preachers, and congregations can help us listen to "here" with guides from traditions other than their own. But, more than multiculturalism, preachers and congregations can begin listening with the multiplicities of biodiverse life that also include multicultural human life.

As we take an inventory of our living traditions, we may begin to find ourselves listening to biologists, activists, and nonreligious community organizers. We may find ourselves listening with students and

---

29. Kwok, *Postcolonial Politics and Theology*, 21.
30. Kwok, *Postcolonial Politics and Theology*, 23.

community gardeners. The poet Camille Dungy describes her process of working against the grain of a home owner's association and transforming her monochromatic yard into a pollinator's paradise. As she nurtures her garden, Dungy—a Black woman living in a predominantly white city—says that thinking about land is, for her, inextricably linked with thinking about the United States' history, and about race. She is constantly reminded of the labor of enslaved Black people who were forced to work the soil, and of the Native Americans forced from their lands. "I can't dig in my garden," she says, "without digging up all this old dirt." Yet that same act of digging in her garden also provides Dungy with welcome relief. For a socially engaged person, she says, "A garden can be a balm." She explains, "A garden can be a place of rest and beauty, and a retreat from that persistent, difficult work. But a garden also teaches me patience, and teaches me that . . . the work of a socially-engaged person often requires true patience. And the garden supports my belief that that patience can very frequently pay off."[31] Dungy inventories the traces of colonialism in her life and listens to the multiplicities of biodiverse life. As she rewilds her domesticated yard, she faces the wounds and gifts of the land.

In responding to the above questions, we may find ourselves listening to environmental refugees, not merely as objects of our concern but as our teachers and prophets. We may also find ourselves listening to leading scientists and marginalized nonconformists. At the border between San Diego and Tijuana, the activist Daniel Watman chained himself to the national border wall in protest of the federal government replacing the eighteen-foot border walls with new thirty-foot border walls near Friendship Park. Watman tends a binational garden along the wall, and as part of the protest, he placed a banner at the garden that read, "Yes, to Friendship! No to walls!" A child was passing by as he was chained to the wall, and Watman explained to the curious child, "I want there to be a park here, not a prison." When work on the new wall was underway, the binational garden was literally uprooted and removed.[32] While the binational garden is itself a form of protest, Watman directly confronts the powers of neocolonial projects that disregard the biodiverse life of local ecosystems, and he accentuates our inattention to ways in which we daily live engulfed by those neocolonial projects. Seth Clark, the pastor of the binational Border Church, commented, "As far as Dan's own spiritual background, Dan tells

---

31. Block, "She Ripped up Her Manicured Lawn," *NPR*, May 5, 2023.
32. Mendoza, "Protestors Chain Themselves to Border Wall."

me that he grew up not following any religion or spiritual path," and Clark continued, "What drew this non-religious person [Dan] to Border Church was his alignment with some of its principles—and of religion in general—without any decision or concerted effort to become religious personally."[33] Clark also has explained that Watman shares what resources he can and builds relationships with people who are temporarily living in canyons near the border.[34] As a nonreligious activist, Watman found common ground with Border Church in their welcoming spirit, weekly communion, and bi-national friendship-building. Having lived in the borderland for more than twenty years,[35] Watman embodies a love for the land and a living critique of neocolonial projects.

In responding to the above questions, what if we find ourselves listening and immersed in community with the more-than-human? What if our teachers and prophets are not only limited to human interlocutors? What if we begin listening and being attentive with a tree or a hillside? Can a tree or a hillside awaken us to depths and horizons of biodiverse life with whom we share community? Wendell Berry described a steep hillside that revealed to him the limits of his own knowledge and a need for changed relationship with the hillside. He wanted the hillside to support livestock with a regular source of water, so he decided to create a small pond on the hillside. He hired a man with a bulldozer to cut into the hillside. The man with the bulldozer cleared away trees and cut into the hillside. Before the bulldozer was finished with the work, water already began seeping into the newly formed bowl to create the pond. The leftover soil was piled up in a curvature on the lower side of the pond. It appeared to be a success. Berry fertilized and planted grass and clover to heal the exposed ground. The following winter turned out to be very wet. The soil froze and thawed. The ground grew heavy and soft. The curvature at the bottom of the pond began to slump, and a slice of soil and trees at the top of the hill slid into the newly formed pond. The problem, he concluded, was a familiar one: "Too much power, too little knowledge." The hillside revealed to him the limits of his knowledge and the need for him to change his relationship with the land. Though he received professional advice for how to proceed in creating the pond on the hillside, the advice he received was not from someone who

---

33. Clark, *Church at the Wall*, 111.
34. Clark, *Church at the Wall*, 110–11.
35. Clark, *Church at the Wall*, 108.

Where to Begin? With Whom?

had local and intimate knowledge of that particular hillside.[36] The wooded hillside was already a functioning biodiverse ecosystem. In the process of cutting into the land, Berry reckoned with his own responsibility for wounding the land.

What if we can learn not only from our mistakes in wounding a particular patch of land but also from life that thrives in the midst of our ruinous mistakes? Anna Lowenhaupt Tsing explores the entangled life of matsutake mushrooms, which are a prized gift in Japan. By describing ways in which plantations in Brazil "exterminated local people and plants" for exploited labor and single cash crops, Tsing shows in contrast how matsutake mushrooms depend on native biodiversity in order to thrive, thriving particularly after human disruptions of forest ecosystems.[37] The land and the people on the land picking the mushrooms are entangled in environmental, economic, political, and historical wounds, propelled into shared spaces by war, displacement, and trauma.[38] The mushrooms and people together create forms of life in the patchwork ruins of capitalism. However, it can often require attentive and trained eyes to recognize signs of life beneath the soil. In Oregon's Cascade Mountains, Tsing accompanied a picker, Kao, who could discern the mushrooms in the soil. Tsing recalled, "In the gathering dark, we scrambled up a rocky hillside not far from his camp. I saw nothing but dirt and some scrawny pine trees. But here was Kao with his bucket and stick, poking deep into clearly empty ground and pulling up a fat button. How could this be possible? There had been nothing there—and then there it was."[39] Searching for signs of life and learning how that burgeoning life creates collaborative ways of being in the ruins of the Anthropocene may be one of the most fundamental responsibilities for preachers. Preachers may learn from mushrooms and the people who forage them. Tsing comments, "If all our forests are buffeted by such winds of destructions, whether capitalists find them desirable or throw them aside, we have the challenge of living in that ruin, ugly and impossible as it is."[40] Mushrooms can be teachers for how to live and even thrive amidst the ruins.

As preachers peer out the window and take a step outside and join a conversation with "here," preachers will witness the whole earth pulsing

---

36. Berry, *What Are People For?*, 5.
37. Tsing, *Mushroom at the End of the World*, 39–40.
38. E.g., Tsing, *Mushroom at the End of the World*, 92.
39. Tsing, *Mushroom at the End of the World*, 14.
40. Tsing, *Mushroom at the End of the World*, 213.

with life. Yet, even as preachers look out beyond the congregation, preachers do not need to lose sight of the congregation. When members of the congregation or spiritual community are given license to engage beyond assumed parameters of piety and use their whole range of experience, the preaching preparation and preaching event will benefit from the local knowledges of biologists, therapists, doctors, students, unhoused neighbors, and "organic intellectuals," each "well-versed in their own wisdom."[41] More than being limited to only human interactions, could a carpenter and a tree, together, be organic intellectuals? On many occasions, over a slice of pizza, church members and I share conversations with groups of college students on the corner of Campanile and Montezuma in the College Area of San Diego. Church members talk about their experience of the neighborhood's evolution over the course of the past thirty-five years—they are friends with local shopkeepers and possess an intimate knowledge of how to navigate the neighborhood. College students reflect on their experiences in the university over the past year—they are current with the latest trends of desire and language. They and we together are part of the Earth's local, "reflexive consciousness."[42] With their contrasting perspectives of place and time, they contribute to my deepening local knowledge, whether or not they are present for the formal preaching event. Preachers may hold the illusion that we are responsible for curating all the local knowledges of "here," when in fact preachers face from the pulpit an ocean of local knowledges in the congregation and surrounding community, constituted by the human and the more-than-human. Listening and being guided by the local knowledges of "here" unfolds within the congregation and beyond.

As our ears are tuned to hear those who are speaking on behalf of local biodiverse ecosystems and those whose homes are being decimated by environmental catastrophe, we will likely begin to find ourselves moving away from monochromatic Eurocentric voices, who have directly and indirectly benefited from colonization and extractivist practices. Theological imagination that has been animated by monochromatic Eurocentric voices needs transformation. What if preachers and congregations listen and draw intersectional guidance from people such as a Yanomami shaman in the Amazon rainforest? In San Diego, what if preachers and congregations listen and learn from local Kumeyaay leaders and communities? What if preachers and congregations listen and follow questions from spiritual but

---

41. Carvalhaes, *Ritual at World's End*, 69.
42. Berry, *Great Work*, 174.

not religious college students? How will our theologies and homiletical practices begin to change? What assumed borders of piety and geography will we transgress? Will fresh emphases within Christian traditions begin to emerge, theological themes and practices that have otherwise resided only on the periphery of homiletical attention? What will we begin to see in biblical texts that have otherwise evaded our hermeneutical gaze? How will the substance and presentation of our preaching evolve?

CONCLUSIONS: TRANSFORMATIONS OF BEING, FEELING, SEEING "HERE"

After he and I enjoyed a delicious supper of nopales tacos with people from Border Church, Cláudio Carvalhaes spoke with Daniel Watman about the binational garden he cultivates along the national border wall in the Tijuana/San Diego region. The garden and the wall represent opposing ways of seeing and inhabiting the world. Carvalhaes reflected on the stark contrast, saying, "I think what we see here is an eventful space where so many things are happening," and he continued gesturing with his hands towards the wall, "We have the wall and what it brings to destroy life. But then we have here with Daniel and this garden the presence of life. So, we see here the resilience of the human and the spirit of the plants resisting." Carvalhaes continued,

> If [the wall] is a sign of our worst demons, then [the garden] is a sign of our best angels, of the possibility of creating beauty.... [The wall] wants to turn everything into one kind of people.... [The garden] wants to celebrate the diversity of the soil and of the plants and of life. And so, what Daniel is doing here is a testimony to all of us for how the human spirit in deep relation with the land can create together different worlds with a sense of beauty and a sense of joy. If [the wall] makes us sick, then [this garden] heals us. And so, this is a testimony of the possibility of new worlds. If [the wall] wants to shut down the world, then [the garden] wants to celebrate the possibility of many worlds together.

The places we occupy and the people who love these places are interwoven. They are not separate. As we learn to see, touch, taste, smell, and hear the places we occupy from the people who love these places, what and how we see will change. What we feel and believe about these places will change. Our relationships with the places we occupy will change. How we tell and write our histories will change. We will no longer merely be asking about source material for preaching or about homiletical authorities. We will no longer be asking for "solutions" to counteract environmental catastrophe, as if our lives can or should continue as they are. Our ways of seeing and being will be transformed. We will be speaking with, from, and for rivers, marshes, trees, and mountains. They will be part of us, and we will be part of them. We will become interwoven, beautifully and tenderly entangled, like trees and fungi nurturing each other's lives. We will cultivate gardens of resistance in desecrated places.

While Howard Thurman described listening for "the sound of the genuine"[43] in yourself and in other people, I realize that part of what I am searching for is "the sound of the genuine" of "here." Finding our way more fully into the places we occupy will no doubt be an ongoing process. Seeing and feeling the multiplicities of life encircling us and animating us will involve a multi-directional transformation of vision. We will need to listen to and learn from traditions and species other than our own, moving beyond Western and Eurocentric theologies and homiletics, moving towards what Sallie McFague has described as a "collegial theological style," an "openness to and appreciation of a variety of passionately held convictions."[44]

Looking out across the Faith Presbyterian Church campus in the College Area, I see a four-way, paved intersection with traffic lights and buses and cars lined up in all four directions. I see asphalt and concrete in every direction with a small patch of grass in the church courtyard. I see apartments and nine-story buildings. I see telephone poles and power lines. I see marks of inherited human cultures, histories, and technologies in every direction. All of this may appear ordinary and normal to my eyes. But, if I begin to take an inventory of the inherited human cultures, histories, and technologies that inform my vision, generative questions may arise. Who and what else do I see here? Whose lives are prioritized in this space? Whose movement is prioritized? The roads intended to make human travel faster and more efficient for funneling students and faculty into buildings also prevent animals, who live in canyons throughout the College Area, to safely roam and search for food. Are there wildlife crossings or green bridges? How is this space habitable for pollinators? In addition to national borders, there are borders that prevent animals from safely traveling are often assumed as natural and necessary.

43. Thurman, "Sound of the Genuine."
44. McFague, *Body of God*, 68, 69.

Where to Begin? With Whom?

As I seek to unlearn my inherited vision, I am reminded of what Carvalhaes told me years ago: "Urgent things must be done slowly." For preachers, unlearning how we see "here" and collaborating with natives of "here" are imperative and urgent tasks. Yet, these tasks are part of a lifelong vocation. Even in small, almost insignificant ways, I have noticed a change in my own field of vision. On many days, as I am walking on the sidewalk between the church campus and the university campus in the College Area, I see the dead bodies of bees strewn across the ground. I had not noticed them before, though I suspect I had been walking by such scenes many times unaware. I have slowly become more attuned to my life being connected with theirs in this urban neighborhood.

When we begin "here," inventory our ways of seeing, and let our vision be transformed, we will encounter and find the people who love "here," now and in the past. The life of "here" will animate our lives and subsequently our sermons. Learning how to be entangled with "here" and the people who have loved "here" will become a lifelong vocation.

PROMPTS FOR PREACHING PREPARATION— ENTERING COMMUNITY "HERE"

If you are customarily inside when you prepare sermons, then look out your window and step outside.

Who is there, not only humans but more-than-human subjects?

Slow down and write down what you see.

Bring the people and place into community, and prepare your sermon with your community "here."

"IN DEEP WATER"[45]

Jonah 1:17–2:10

One afternoon this past week, I was walking through this sanctuary, and I looked across the courtyard. Truth be told, no matter what day or time of day, many things happen in this courtyard, some of them you would hardly

---

45. I preached this sermon on September 17, 2023, at Faith Presbyterian Church, San Diego.

believe. I looked across the courtyard, and a barefooted, middle-aged man wearing beekeeper's gear was walking briskly across the grass. He looked like a man on a mission, eyes clear and piercing, with something on his mind.

I walked outside and over to him and said, "Do you love bees?" Those were the first words that stumbled out of my mouth to a complete stranger.

And, he said, "Yes, I love bees. I know God's purpose for my life, and it feels good."

And those were those first words that shot out of his mouth.

So, I said, "Right, let me show you the beehive."

He said, "Great, let's take a look."

And, of course, I was smiling all the way, as we walked to the countless bees swarming all over the place.

This past week, we had an issue with multitudes of bees in the preschool playground. As it would turn out, a whole hive of bees had been growing right under our noses without us knowing. So, we called someone to relocate the bees to a more appropriate location.

I have been thinking all week about what he said: "I know God's purpose for my life, and it feels good." Maybe he said that because he knew I am a pastor, and he was simply trying to tell me what he thought I wanted to hear. But, in my estimation, he seemed entirely and disarmingly genuine.

When we align ourselves with the deepest longing God has placed within our hearts, we will find ourselves brimming with joy. That joy is a gift. That joy is a sign of God's presence in our lives. There's more to the beekeeper's story, and I will come back to him later.

Jonah, on the other hand, does everything he can to flee from the calling God has placed within his heart. God sends Jonah across the land, east, to Nineveh, but Jonah goes to the sea, west, as far away from Nineveh as imaginable. Jonah runs away because he hates the people of Nineveh; the people of Nineveh were likely on the verge of invading Jonah's people. God was sending Jonah to the place that Jonah least wanted to go.

In *scene three* of Jonah's story, Jonah finds himself in deep water. This moment may very well be the most familiar moment of the whole story, perhaps one of the most familiar scenes of the whole Bible. This scene has captivated the imaginations of every Sunday school child and countless generations: Jonah and the big fish. This is a turning point for Jonah, a literal change of direction.

Where to Begin? With Whom?

After the sailors hurl Jonah overboard into the raging sea, God speaks to a fish. And God sends the fish in Jonah's direction, and the fish swallows Jonah. Commentators have sometimes interpreted the fish as God's grace in Jonah's life. The fish rescues Jonah from the storm, and then Jonah launches into a prayer of gratitude from inside the fish.

The novelist Aldous Huxley creatively imagined Jonah inside the fish. Huxley wrote,

> Seated upon the convex mound
> Of one vast kidney Jonah prays
> And sings his canticles and hymns.
> Making the hollow vault resound
> God's goodness and mysterious ways
> Til
> The great fish spouts music as he swims.[46]

Huxley imagined that the giant fish became like a cathedral, echoing with Jonah's gratitude and praise.

Scene three of Jonah's story begins and ends with the giant fish. But most of this scene is a psalm, a prayer of gratitude to God. Over and over, in this prayer, Jonah describes that he is on the brink of death. We read that Jonah was in the fish for *three days*. According to some ancient traditions, three days was the length of time it would take to travel to the underworld, the land of the dead. In other words, Jonah was traveling toward death. Over and over in this prayer, Jonah poetically describes himself facing death. "Out of the belly of Sheol," "into the heart of the seas," "deep surrounded me," "my life was ebbing away."[47] And, in the throes of this journey into death, Jonah gives thanks to God for saving him from death. Jonah exclaims, "You heard my voice," "you brought up my life from the Pit," "Deliverance belongs to the Lord!" So, in a way, you might say that it is as Huxley imagined, the belly of the fish, the depths of disaster, are transformed into a cathedral, echoing with Jonah's gratitude.

It is interesting to me that while he was on land, Jonah runs away; when he was on the boat, Jonah was asleep, completely indifferent to everyone and everything; when Jonah felt that he was in control of his life, he fled God's call on his life like a plague. When he thought he was in control, he tried to do whatever he wanted, and he was indifferent to whatever he didn't want. But when he was caught up in catastrophe, after he had lost all

---

46. As cited by Limburg, *Hosea to Micah*, 146.
47. Limburg, *Hosea to Micah*, 147.

semblance of control, Jonah prays. This is important. In catastrophe, Jonah experiences a *slight* change of heart, perhaps not entirely; but the callousness around his heart has begun to crack. God's merciful love has touched and softened his heart.[48]

The Spanish mystic Teresa of Avila said, "God's love thaws the holy in us."[49] Jonah's cold, hard heart has begun to thaw, to soften ever so slightly. It is often the case that when we are comfortable, we may hardly even think of prayer; prayer appears utterly useless; prayer seems like a waste of time. But when we are the ones in desperate need of support and help, when we feel that everything is spiraling out of control, we call out to anyone who will listen, hoping with our whole heart, more honest than we usually dare to be, that God will consider our circumstances, that anyone will hear us. That's Jonah—and that's probably most of us, but that's not advisable. Jonah's road map is not a good road map to follow. I would not recommend waiting to pray until catastrophe falls into our lives.

But, as I think about this for myself, I think the good news, here, is that even if we *do* follow a similar road to Jonah—running from our calling as quickly as we possibly can, not softening our hearts until catastrophe falls into our lives—even if we do follow such a road of resistance, keeping our hearts cold, God does not abandon us. God stays right there with us.

The beekeeper I met this past week said to me, "I know God's purpose for my life, and it feels good." There is more to his story. He explained to me that he had been an emergency medical technician (an EMT) for a while, and he had planned to be a firefighter. But, for various reasons, the fire department did not want him. And then he discovered bees, and he fell in love. He's been a beekeeper ever since.

Think about this. He discovered his life's calling by *not* being able to go in the direction he was trying to go. Our lives may *not* unfold how we anticipate. We may very well find ourselves in places and circumstances that we could not have planned and that we would not have chosen for ourselves. But even when we find ourselves in the depths, we may find a gift, grace given to us by God.

The professor of literature Joseph Campbell said, "Where you stumble, there lies your treasure. The very cave you are afraid to enter turns out to be the source of what you are looking for. The . . . thing in the cave, that was so

---

48. Stuart, *Hosea to Jonah*, 472–73.
49. As cited by Boyle, *Forgive Everyone Everything*, 43.

dreaded, has become the centre."[50] Stumbling may not be a waste of time at all. Stumbling may actually draw our attention to what we otherwise could not have seen but needed to see. What we most fear may simply be what we do not yet understand but need to understand. When you are afraid, slow down.

God saves Jonah from the storm. God also saves Jonah from himself. God saves Jonah from his own cold heart, or at least, God begins to thaw, to soften Jonah's heart. Could this be the first hint of transformation in Jonah? Mind you, Jonah's heart was not entirely there yet. But this moment in the story is a beginning of transformation.

The fish spits Jonah onto dry land, back to the land of the living. The fish changes Jonah's direction. This was a turning point for Jonah. And then, Jonah proceeds, begrudgingly, by going to the place he does not wish to go; Jonah goes to the place he probably fears to go; he goes to the place he does not understand. He goes to the place he needs to go.

Everything in us may be resisting; fear may be coursing through our body; nothing about our direction may seem to make sense. We do not need to be the ones in control. We need simply to let our hearts thaw, to let our hearts soften to the possibility that God desires to offer mercy and love. Sometimes, it is precisely in unexpected circumstances or an unexpected friendship that we discover our deepest calling, that we discover an unexpected gift, that we find God has been with us all along. Much of the time, God does not send a fish to change our direction and soften our heart. Many times, at least in my experience, God sends a person or a circumstance.

Almost three years ago, I began working with Claudio Carvalhaes, a Brazilian American liberation theologian. I was working on a project about how white supremacy infects worship in white American churches. He agreed to work with me, but he said that he would challenge me all the way. Carvalhaes is a preeminent liberation theologian who teaches at a seminary in New York City. He has written books in English and Portuguese. Several years ago, he traveled four continents listening and praying with some of the most marginalized and most violently exploited people in the world. With them, he wrote prayers. He turned their prayers into a book to share with all of us. And, just recently, he has written a play that will be featured in the New York City Theatre Festival next month. So, as you can imagine, almost three years ago, when he agreed to work with me, I was simply

---

50. As cited by Ó Tuama, *In the Shelter*.

happy to have the chance. Little did I know how working with him would change my life.

At a certain point, perhaps two years ago, as we were talking on Zoom, he began challenging me to turn my attention to the life of plants and insects and biodiversity of all kinds. I was trying to write about worship in a violently racialized America. I felt that my project was already growing way beyond what I had ever intended. So, in all my wisdom, I said with profound insight, "If I do that, my project will turn into a balloon." And he said, "This is not a balloon! All of our lives depend on changing our relationship with the earth." So, I began paying attention, or, at least, trying to, in small ways. I began paying attention to the life of trees and moss and insects and animals and nearly any form of life.

On one occasion, I was running at the Mission Trails Regional Park, and I almost stepped on a common pinacate beetle. But, instead of stepping on it or running around it, I stopped. I flipped it over onto its legs with my index finger, and it scurried away. This was a gestalt switch for me, a change in perspective and a turning point for me. You may think that is hardly saving the *planet*, but I was beginning to pay attention to all the biodiversity around me. And *that* was saving *me*. And then I remembered something Carvalhaes had told to me: "Unless you are transformed, no one around you will be transformed." That's when I realized that *I* was on a journey of transformation. It wasn't only about the project anymore.

Fast-forward three years, to this past week, and I found myself stepping into a twenty-dollar beekeeper's costume to save a beehive in the preschool playground. If you have been wondering why I have been speaking so much about our relationship with the Earth, why we have spent all year talking about trees and bees, why several church women's groups were talking about bees a week ago, and why I wanted to rescue rather than kill a multitude of bees in the preschool playground, you have Carvalhaes to thank for that. And next year, in February, you can thank him yourself, because he will be visiting us here at Faith.

To be clear, I am not saying that I am Jonah and Carvalhaes is a giant fish, but I am saying that he has helped me change direction and soften my heart.

Sometimes, it is precisely in unexpected circumstances or an unexpected friendship that we discover our deepest calling, that we discover an unexpected gift, that we find God has been with us all along.

Where to Begin? With Whom?

"LEARNING TO WEEP: LOSS, LAMENT, AND GRIEF"[51]

Luke 19:41–44

Jesus draws near, sees the city, and weeps. This moment is palpable to me. I can feel it. His heart was entangled with that city. He grew up visiting there as a child with his parents. He had the audacity to teach the teachers, even when he was young. And now, in Luke's Gospel, he knows this is where he will be killed in a system and by a people who destroy their most vulnerable neighbors.

As his heart breaks, he weeps and says, "If you had only recognized the things that make for peace." I chose this text for today several months ago. I have been pondering what this text, this moment in Luke's Gospel, means for me, personally.

I have come to read this text as an invitation to inventory the losses I have experienced, the unarticulated laments that I carry in my heart, and the grief I hold in my body. This public acknowledgment of grief does not feel natural to me as someone with a Scots-Irish Presbyterian heritage, raised to be impassive, unexpressive with my emotions.

To begin today, I want to offer an invitation for us, here, today. We may or may not give much time to considering the losses we experience, the unarticulated laments we carry, or the grief our bodies hold. We may very well be rushing around attempting to offer whatever pastoral help we can with and for people and places around us. But, today, I want to offer some time for us to do an inventory in our own lives.

Here is your invitation. Think of the first time you wept or an early memory you hold of weeping. Hold on to that memory. It is sacred. It will be a guide for you on your journey of tenderness[52] and entanglement. Pay attention to the connections.

A few months ago, my eight-year-old son Ezra and I were sitting on the couch at home, and he asked me, "Daddy, have you ever cried before?" I said, "Yes, I have cried before." And then Ezra said, "I have never seen you cry". He paused, and then said, "Next time you cry, tell me, so I can see."

---

51. I preached this sermon on February 17, 2024, for the San Diego Presbytery Leadership Day in San Diego.

52. Gutierrez comments, "Without love and affection, without—why not say it?—tenderness, there can be no true gesture of solidarity." *We Drink from Our Own Wells*, 104.

His comment touched deeper than he ever could have known. Ten years ago, I was a hospital chaplain resident sitting in the on-call room when I received a call at two in the morning. A baby had been born several months premature and did not survive. The mother and father requested a chaplain. At that time of night, I was the only one available. I entered the room. I saw the mother holding the baby in the palm of her hand. I had no words. I introduced myself, and we sat together for awhile. Eventually, I offered a feeble attempt at a prayer, and shortly thereafter, I returned to the on-call room. I sat on the edge of the bed in the on-call room, and I *tried* to cry. I wanted to cry. But no tears came. I felt like something must be broken inside of me.

Often our private life tangles with our public and professional life. At that same time, as I was visiting this young couple after losing their child, my wife and I really wanted to have a child, and it wasn't happening.

About a week later, I was called to the neonatal intensive care unit in the hospital. I was asked to administer a baptism for a baby girl before they removed life support. That was my first baptism as a pastor.

I was falling apart. It was at that point—May 2014—that I considered quitting the hospital chaplain residency. But, with the support of peers and a gracious supervisor, I finished the year.

Ezra's comment, "I have never seen you cry," touched me deeper than he ever could have known.

One of the earliest memories I hold of weeping is from when I was ten years old. I was with my parents and siblings; we were driving up to Front Royal, Virginia, to visit my aunt and uncle. I loved visiting them because my uncle would take hours out of his day and build model airplanes with me. When we arrived at their house, it was empty and quiet. They were returning from an air show. My uncle Jeff was a pilot flying a World War II plane, a P-38.

Shortly after we arrived to the empty house, the phone rang. My mom answered. The quiet of the house collapsed into a deeper silence. I entered the room where my mom was on the phone. My mom looked at me and, eventually, she told me my uncle died in a plane crash. He had died on impact.

I suddenly realized he was gone. I would not see him again. My body betrayed me. Tears flowed down my cheeks. I collapsed into a couch and curled into a ball. I don't remember for how long I stayed there weeping. Ten years old.

Where to Begin? With Whom?

He spent hours with me building model airplanes, carefully painting and gluing the pieces. When he was gone, I tried to build my own model airplanes and model ships, but they never turned out the same. I always wanted to rush to the end. I never wanted to paint the pieces first.

I have been doing an inventory of the losses I have experienced, the unarticulated laments that I carry in my heart, and the grief I hold in my body. I am holding on to these memories. They are sacred. They are guides for me on my journey of tenderness and entanglement.

The theologian Willie Jennings has traced the contours of colonization and the European missionary movements that assisted colonization. In 1854, the Cambridge-educated Anglican missionary bishop John William Colenso arrived at the colony of Natal in what is now South Africa. He entered a colonizing space fragmented by the settler colonizer's desire, disrupting Indigenous practices and commodifying all aspects of life, land, animals, and people.[53] Colenso joined the colonizing process as a missionary. Willie Jennings has observed that eventually, "Colenso came to feel pathos for the Africans who were called and treated as nonhuman. This, finally, is Christian translation. And such translation cost Bishop Colenso everything."[54] Colenso began to feel pathos, and that pathos was the path to translation. He began to feel and see the world and people other than his own as worthy of moral regard.

Pathos opens our hearts for connection. In order to understand another person and place, I need to feel not only my own pain, but I need to be able to feel another person's pain. An inventory of our early memories of grief can be guides in feeling the places we occupy. Where are our hearts most tender? How do the tender places in our hearts connect with the places we occupy?

I have wondered why the testimony of Davi Kopenawa, a Yanomami shaman in the Amazon rainforest, touches me so deeply, when he speaks of the destruction of the rainforest, the destruction of his home. We live in a time of countless catastrophes. Why is it that Davi Kopenawa touches my heart so profoundly? Eventually, I have come to realize that, of course, as a child, trees towered over me and encircled me every day. The trees were and still are dear to me, to say nothing of that fact that all of our lives utterly depend on trees. So, of course, when Davi Kopenawa describes the

---

53. Jennings, *Christian Imagination*, 123–24.
54. Jennings, *Christian Imagination*, 166.

destruction of the rainforest it touches me, profoundly—he touches a tender place in my heart, he touches the heart of my childhood home.

An estimated 80 percent of the rainforest that is being destroyed is being destroyed for cattle grazing—for raising meat for consumers.[55] So, here I am entangled in a system and with a people that devours the most vulnerable people and places on the planet. What do I do with that?

In my case, as a preacher, I invited our church here to spend a year becoming more attentive to our relationship with the Earth. I spent two months preaching about the symbolic and literal significance of trees. If you think I am crazy, then you are perhaps a rational person. But I am not trying to be only a rational person. But, remember, the Bible begins and ends with trees.

To my surprise, parishioners would sometimes share with me how grateful they were, even with tears streaking down their cheeks. That is deep calling to deep, one heart speaking to another. I found my heart connecting with the land, and my heart connecting with the people around me.

We may or may not think or feel that we have time to inventory the losses we experience, the unarticulated laments we carry, or the grief our bodies hold. But, today, I want to offer some time for us to do that together. To quote our guest, Dr. Cláudio Carvalhaes, "To care is to learn *how* to be entangled."[56]

So, let early memories of grief guide your heart into deeper tenderness and entanglement. Pay attention to the connections that your grief brings to light. And most importantly, do this not only for your own sake, but for the sake of your churches and communities and the life of the Earth. Where are the tender places in your heart? How do the tender places in your heart connect with the places you occupy?

San Diego Presbytery is a borderland presbytery. Do we feel the wounds of the borderland? If we do not, then why not?

In just a moment, as we sing our second hymn together, you are invited to light a candle. Light a candle as you recall an early memory of grief, from your childhood or other moment in your life.

Begin to take an inventory of the losses you have experienced, the unarticulated laments that you carry in your heart, and the grief you hold in your body. Be attentive to ways in which these tender places in your heart connect with the land you occupy.

---

55. Figueres and Rivett-Carnac, *Future We Choose*, 124.
56. Carvalhaes, *How Do We Become Green People and Earth Communities?*, 112.

CHAPTER 4

Toward a Homiletics of Entanglement

"We have to change our whole
relationship with the Earth."[1]

THÍCH NHẤT HẠNH

"Ecologize all that we do and think."[2]

LEONARDO BOFF

"'We' are ecosystems that span boundaries and
transgress categories. Our selves emerge from
a complex tangle of relationships."[3]

MERLIN SHELDRAKE

"To care is to learn how to be entangled."[4]

CLÁUDIO CARVALHAES

"But ask the animals, and they will teach you,
the birds of the air, and they will tell you;
ask the plants of the earth, and they will teach you,
and the fish of the sea will declare to you."[5]

JOB 12:7–8

1. Hạnh, *Love Letter to the Earth*, 10.
2. Boff, *Cry of the Earth, Cry of the Poor,* 13.
3. Sheldrake, *Entangled Life*, 18.
4. Carvalhaes, *How Do We Become Green People and Earth Communities?*, 112.
5. NRSVUE.

Searching for Speech

Having already preached scrappy sermons in the context of church worship services for years, I eagerly walked through the door of my first homiletics class at Fuller Theological Seminary in Pasadena, California. I hungered to learn how to preach properly. I will always be indebted to the excellent instruction I received from my preaching professors at Fuller. I have since wondered, however, about the craft of preaching I practiced at Fuller, whether it remained an anthropocentric intellectual exercise removed from the life of the Earth.

For my first preaching practicum, I delivered two sermons and listened to my peers deliver sermons. I preached behind a podium in a small classroom with no windows and no possibility of sunlight in the room. For my second preaching practicum, I delivered two more sermons and then listened to my peers deliver sermons. I preached behind a podium in a small classroom with modest-sized windows and the shades drawn. There was no sunlight in the room. I was untroubled by the classroom setting at the time. It seemed normal to me. However, since my days in seminary, I have begun a journey of unlearning how to preach, unlearning some of what I implicitly gathered about the craft of preaching.

A preacher is not a solitary individual proclaiming good news to polite listeners, who sit quietly in their seats until the preacher finishes expositing a biblical text, in a room with the shades drawn, removed from the daily pressures of the world. A preacher is not a biblical exegete disconnected from the realities of environmental catastrophe. A preacher is entangled with all the realities that touch and animate the listeners' lives,[6] and the listeners are not only the subdued humans sitting in chairs facing toward the preacher. A preacher is involved with all the beings—human and more-than-human—who are present, and therefore, a preacher has a responsibility for the news that leaves their lips to be good for all those who are present, from the smallest ant scurrying across the carpeted floor to the largest oak towering over the building, until their preaching proclaims the gospel that "encompasses the cosmos."[7]

We need full-bodied speech. To find ourselves as preachers entangled is to bear witness to the networks of relations that constitute our lives as members of the Earth's life. We are entangled in pernicious forms of

---

6. Justo L. González and Catherine G. González argue, "Connection is the task of preaching" an "interweaving of text, occasion, historical setting, and the life of the preacher." *Liberating Pulpit*, 110, 118.

7. Gaventa, *When In Romans*, 128.

Toward a Homiletics of Entanglement

exploitation, and we are entangled in life-giving systems of biodiverse community. In what ways can our sermons embody the many entanglements—cultural, economic, political, biological, social—that characterize our lives? Trees, soils, bees, humans, and material exchanges are not commodities but are sacred relations, each worthy of moral and homiletical attention.[8] Developing a homiletics of entanglement may involve moving away from the view of a preacher as an expert individual and toward a view of a preacher as someone akin to a tree, networked with fungi to many communities of trees and forms of biodiverse life. While facing the harsh winds of white supremacy, capitalism, and colonization, a preacher, as Hyeran Kim-Cragg describes, can become "like a bamboo tree, supple enough to bend but strong enough not to be broken."[9] Moreover, as someone akin to a tree in a community of biodiverse life, a preacher is no longer alone as an individual expert; every living body and being becomes part of the preaching event.

At the end of this chapter, I include prompts for preaching preparation, and I offer a sermon that seeks to bring the congregation playfully into the preaching event. Many in the congregation, including children and adults, were invited to wear black and yellow bee antennae. As the preaching event unfolded, they found themselves involved in the message of the sermon. This chapter may prove most useful by reading the sermon at the end of the chapter first, reading the chapter, and then rereading the sermon.

In this chapter, by "a homiletics of entanglement," I mean a theory and practice of preaching that arises from local, biodiverse environments of a spiritual community in conversation with biblical texts. A homiletics of entanglement will follow insights from postcolonial praxis and ecological theology (ecotheology) in order to move toward an ecological homiletics (ecohomiletics). A homiletics of entanglement will explicitly grapple with the pernicious entanglements of the West and will seek to promote life-giving entanglements in local, biodiverse community.[10] A homiletics of

---

8. While reflecting on Switzerland's Constitution, which provides protections for "the dignity of creation when handling animals, plants, and other organisms," the German forester Peter Wohlleben has said, "I, for one, welcome breaking down the moral barriers between animals and plants." See *Hidden Life of Trees*, 244. Larry Rasmussen develops what he describes as an "earth-honoring ethic" in which we shift "from the ego to the ecosphere as the center of moral attention and method." *Earth-Honoring Faith*, 223.

9. Kim-Cragg, *Postcolonial Preaching*, 4.

10. Rob Nixon has noted that postcolonial theory draws attention to displacement and conservationist movements focus on local place, *Slow Violence*, 238–39. Moreover, Gilio-Whitaker has observed that conservationist movements have caused the displacement of Indigenous peoples, commenting, "With the birth of the conservation and

entanglement will invite participants in the preaching event into an alternative consciousness.[11] One of the keys will be to learn *how* to be entangled with many forms of relations in life-affirming and life-giving ways through the course of preparing and preaching sermons in biodiverse community. Three concepts—biomimicry, collective effervescence, polyphonies—will gesture toward learning how to be entangled and will move postcolonial preaching toward an ecohomiletics.

QUESTIONS FOR REFLECTION IN PREPARATION FOR THIS CHAPTER—PRACTICING HOMILETICAL ENTANGLEMENT

Where and in what state is your body when you write/prepare sermons, inside or outside, stationary or moving?

Who are the primary subjects and models in your sermons and how are they related with their biodiverse environments?

In what ways can your sermon center biodiverse life and invite the congregation into learning from the intelligence of the Earth?

What are ways to integrate your congregation's participation into the preaching event and into your sermon's message?

What sounds or voices do your sermons feature in the preaching event?

What are ways you might transgress the assumed etiquette of your context in order to vivify the message of your sermon?

---

national parks movement in the mid-1800's, tribal peoples continued to be pushed out of their homes, fueled by the theory of Manifest Destiny and the view that Indians were an impediment to progress." *As Long As Grass Grows,* 48. A homiletics of entanglement will need to be open-ended in its ongoing recognition of and commitment to understanding (dis)placement and locality.

11. Walter Brueggemann has asserted, "*The task of prophetic ministry is to nurture, nourish, and evoke consciousness and perception alternative to the consciousness and perception of the dominant culture around us.*" *Prophetic Imagination,* 13 (emphasis original). In connecting the roles of the prophet and preacher, Brueggemann has stated, "The poet/prophet is a voice that shatters settled reality and evokes new possibility in the listening assembly." *Finally Comes the Poet,* 4.

Postcolonial Preaching: Creating a Subversive Event

Kwok Pui-Lan offers several insights for postcolonial preaching, which are vital for preaching in the Anthropocene. Kwok explains, "I would portray postcolonial preaching as a locally rooted and globally conscious performance that seeks to create a Third Space so that the faith community can imagine new ways of being in the world and encountering God's salvific action for the oppressed and marginalized," and she continues, "Since the aim of postcolonial preaching is to create a subversive Third Space, the preacher must dislodge the audience from common sense (which usually serves the status quo) and challenge the legacy of colonialism and the logic of empire."[12] If sermons are locally rooted, then a sermon preached in one location may not be preached somewhere else without losing some of its intelligibility. The locality will animate its rationale and trajectory. Moreover, a preacher can identify and trouble assumed etiquette in a space, whether it is unspoken cultural or homiletical etiquette. Eurocentrism can be discarded. The Third Space Kwok indicates involves creating a space that does not yet exist, that pushes against an oppressive status quo, and that the spiritual community begins to embody. "Those who are not given voice by society," she explains, "should be given the space and empowered to share their stories of God's action in their midst."[13] A preacher alongside a spiritual community can discern the voices together that may not be given voice in society and even in their own community. A preacher and spiritual community create a subversive space together.

Part of creating a Third Space in which a preacher transgresses assumed etiquette can include understanding preaching as performance. Understanding preaching as performance will move beyond simply being attentive to the use of narrative structure, rhythm, cadence, and delivery. Preaching as performance will be attentive to a variety of sources across genres, from street theater to mixed media.[14] Preaching as performance will not remain limited to a monologue behind a pulpit or on a stage. Justo L. Gonzalez observes, "Most Hispanics do not see the sermon as a text, but rather as an event."[15] By understanding preaching as performance and as

12. Kwok, *Postcolonial Politics and Theology*, 157.
13. Kwok, *Postcolonial Politics and Theology*, 158.
14. Kwok, *Postcolonial Politics and Theology*, 160.
15. As cited by Kwok Pui-Lan, *Postcolonial Politics and Theology*, 160. Justo L. González and Catherine G. González note, "Preaching is not an event in itself—the sermon—but is rather the midwife of an event—the liturgy, the total act of worship. The

an event, preachers can begin to experiment with forms of performance that transgress the status quo of a worship space and spiritual community.

In a sermon entitled "Walking Barefoot Every Day," I preached on the Exodus text in which Moses encounters a burning bush and the voice of God.[16] The voice tells Moses to take off his sandals because the ground he is standing on is holy. In the middle of the sermon, I stepped out of the pulpit, walked down from the stage to the floor, took off my shoes and socks, and said, "Every step we take is on holy ground." I put my bare feet in contact with the ground. I continued preaching and finished the sermon barefoot while standing on the floor of the sanctuary. I was experimenting with the act and event of preaching itself. I was bringing more of myself and my body into the performance of preaching, and I was tampering with the etiquette of preaching in that space.[17] Taking off shoes and socks in the middle of a sermon is not expected, nor is it ordinarily considered appropriate in my context. I was also inviting listeners to slow down, pay attention to the literal ground beneath our feet, and notice the historical reality of environmental catastrophe that we face. Topsoil is rapidly disappearing, and our lives depend on rich topsoil to grow food. The preaching event turned our attention to our bodies' relationship with the land.

Postcolonial preaching creates "a multivocal and dialogical faith community committed to justice."[18] Kwok Pui-Lan notes, "In urban global cities, it is increasingly common to have church members speaking different mother tongues and immigrants who struggle with English or another colonial language."[19] Images and metaphors will carry varied meaning within the faith community. "In traditional homiletical theory," Kwok Pui-Lan explains, "language is seen as transparent and meaning as stable. The task of the preacher is to impart to listeners the claim of the scriptural text or

---

sermon points to the current historical setting in which the congregation lives its daily lives and in which the liturgy is set, with its pain and injustice; with its yearnings and hopes." *Liberating Pulpit*, 119.

16. Exodus 3:1–12.

17. Myers asserts, "In performing the sermon, we incarnate the gospel. This calls upon preachers to think deeply about the oral and visual dynamics of our preaching," and he says, "We also ought to find creative ways to use our gendered, racialized, sexually oriented, and variously abled bodies in ways that call out for just and equitable valuation of *all* bodies. . . . Our bodies, in other words, can become sites of holy mischief, wreaking havoc on the systems and structures that try to restrict our capacities for being and behaving." *Stand-Up Preaching*, 169, 182.

18. Kwok, *Postcolonial Politics and Theology*, 165.

19. Kwok, *Postcolonial Politics and Theology*, 165.

a message from God. In postcolonial preaching, preaching is a communal event, with the congregation participating and responding."[20] A preacher's mother tongue will no longer be the assumed and dominant language of the space. The variety of languages and cultural norms can inform the preaching event, and the variety can begin to create fresh meanings and possibilities within a spiritual community. As multiplicities of language and cultural norms interact, a spiritual community may begin to face assumed norms that were oppressive but not perceived as oppressive. Practicing a multivocal faith can be a vital aspect of forming a subversive Third Space.

Kwok Pui-Lan offers vital insights for preaching in the Anthropocene. Postcolonial preaching creates subversive space that privileges marginalized voices. Postcolonial preaching performs the values of subversion by moving beyond a monologue behind a pulpit or on a stage and moving into preaching as an event that draws from a variety of nontraditional homiletical sources. Postcolonial preaching creates an event with a spiritual community's diversity of language and culture.

A word with regard to sermon patterns may also prove helpful.[21] Postcolonial preaching gives priority to lived experience; the historical and cultural positioning of a preacher and faith community who bear the marks of colonialism set the trajectory for the preaching event. No single preaching pattern will be used at all times, whether that pattern be expository,[22] inductive,[23] narrative,[24] or otherwise.[25] HyeRan Kim-Cragg observes, "A postcolonial preaching pattern incorporates other patterns,"[26] and she continues, "A postcolonial preaching pattern seeks a method of drawing water, which is consistent with the source of the water. In other words, the how and the what of the message must work together."[27] The lived experience of a preacher and a spiritual community in relation with colonial wounds will shape the patterns of the preaching event, and as assumed etiquette for the preaching event develops in a spiritual community, the etiquette may

---

20. Kwok, *Postcolonial Politics and Theology*, 167.

21. Augustine of Hippo argued that "every variety of style should be introduced." *On Christian Doctrine*, 164.

22. See Long, *Witness of Preaching*.

23. See Craddock, *Preaching*. See also McClure, *Other-Wise Preaching*, 50–51.

24. See Lowry, *How to Preach a Parable*.

25. See McClure, *Other-Wise Preaching*.

26. Kim-Cragg, *Postcolonial Preaching*, 9.

27. Kim-Cragg, *Postcolonial Preaching*, 67.

at times need to be transgressed and unsettled for the sake of creating new possibilities of depth and belonging.[28]

More, however, than arising only from diverse human life, a homiletics of entanglement will draw a preacher and spiritual community into the local, biodiverse life of the Earth. Part of what can contribute to the subversive, performative, and multivocal preaching event will be tracing time and place in terms of the more-than-human ecosystem, breaking open anthropocentrism with multiple centers of biodiverse life.[29] What if ants and trees and coral reefs and hummingbirds' voices are the marginalized voices of the biodiverse community? How will the human spiritual community privilege their voices? What if the lives of bees teach a preacher and spiritual community how to perform life-affirming values in relationship with the Earth? What if the life of trees challenges the cultural norms of a spiritual community's assumed norms of capitalism? The preaching event will invite the whole spiritual community into observing and practicing life-affirming relations within the local ecosystem.

ECOTHEOLOGY: LISTENING WITH THE CRY OF THE EARTH

Traces of ecotheology run throughout the entirety of this book.[30] However, it is worth noting key elements of ecotheology directly in order to animate postcolonial praxis with insights from ecotheology. "Ecology," Leonardo Boff says, "starts with the cry of the Earth, of living things, of the forests, watercourses, soil and air attacked by the type of unlimited material growth promoted by the dominant worldview."[31] Boff describes ecology as "a knowledge of the relations, interconnections, interdependencies, and exchanges of all with all, at all points, and at all moments."[32] Ecotheology,

---

28. McClure notes, "In other-wise preaching, the entire discourse situation is constantly being ruptured or broken open by the preaching event." *Other-Wise Preaching*, 150.

29. I draw inspiration here from Carvalhaes in his description of "multinaturalism" in *Ritual at World's End*, 164–65.

30. Panentheism is a theological position held by some ecotheologians. Leah Schade turns to "*panentheism* as a way to emphasize God's immanence in Creation while retaining God's transcendence and distinction from Creation. This position holds that Creation is part of God but does not constitute the whole of God." *Creation-Crisis Preaching*, 27.

31. Boff, *Thoughts and Dreams of an Old Theologian*, 97.

32. Boff, *Cry of the Earth, Cry of the Poor*, 3.

then, is a not a separate theological discipline. Rather, it is a theological methodology that pays attention to all the wounded connections across all of life. "[Ecology] is a knowledge," Boff says, "of interrelated knowledges.... Ecology embodies an ethical concern likewise drawn from all knowledges, powers, and institutions: to what extent is each individual collaborating to protect nature, which is in jeopardy?"[33] Just as physics, geology, oceanography, biology, anthropology, and philosophy should contribute to protecting and serving the well-being of the whole planet, so too should theology and homiletics contribute to protecting and serving the well-being of the whole planet. It is "imperative to ecologize all that we do and think, to reject closed ideas, mistrust one-way causality, to strive to be inclusive in the face of all exclusions, to be unifying in the face of all disjunctions, to take a holistic approach in the face of all reductionisms, and to appreciate complexity in the face of all oversimplifications."[34] All of life is interconnected. An ecotheology pays attention to connections across all fields, drawing from the wells of Christian theology and homiletics in service of the well-being of the Earth, which is the common good of all species, human and more-than-human.

Cláudio Carvalhaes asserts the importance of the Earth as a guide for Christian theology, as he explains, "If, in the Christian communities what was at stake was the relation between prayers and beliefs and ways of living, this foundation now needs to be guided and reorganized by *lex naturae*. Without this law, no other brilliant theological concept will survive the Anthropocene," and he continues, "*Lex naturae* is not about the protection of religions or traditions but mainly, and most importantly, the protection and restitution of the well-being of the entire world." *Lex naturae* can be an organizing guide for Christian theology and homiletics. What is good for the Earth is good for the church, and what is good for the church must be good for the Earth. Moreover, "Are [our sermons] Earth-honoring?"[35] A preacher has a responsibility to proclaim the wisdom of the Earth.

Sallie McFague traces an alignment between the Christian theological theme of Christ's *kenosis* (self-emptying)[36] and biological evolution. "Trinitarian Christianity and nature," she says, "share a common

---

33. Boff, *Cry of the Earth, Cry of the Poor*, 3–4.
34. Boff, *Cry of the Earth, Cry of the Poor*, 13.
35. Rasmussen, *Earth-Honoring Ethics*, 220.
36. Cf. Philippians 2:1–11.

characteristic—intrinsic relationality."[37] She identifies the ongoing self-sacrificial love of the Triune God as a pattern within evolution—death of self makes new life possible.[38] She asserts, "The kenotic story of Jesus (and God) is a fitting instrument for helping us react positively to the 'turning point' presented by climate change."[39] She seeks to provide an alternative to the myth of the Western individual, who is "Western, young, male, white-skinned, well-to-do, educated, confident, Protestant, able-bodied,"[40] by describing the life of the Trinity most vividly revealed in Jesus as self-emptying love, love that dies so that others might have life. *Kenosis* is "how the universe operates (says evolution), and it is how divinity operates (says the Trinity)."[41] By noticing an alignment between the self-emptying dance of the Trinity and the self-emptying processes of evolution, McFague seeks to show that the pattern of self-emptying is the pattern of reality. The self-emptying dance of the Trinity and of biological evolution belong together. "God and the world," McFague says, "are intrinsically entangled with one another, but God and the world are also separate."[42] The life of the Earth is within the life of God.

The Trinitarian pattern of self-emptying is a pattern Christians can and should follow especially in a time of environmental catastrophe. McFague says,

> God loves the neighbor, loves all others, and we humans are invited to join the cosmic dance of receiving and giving that is, at the same time, the action of the Trinity—and, at another level, also the action of evolution. Hence we see a hidden truth emerging here in both the Trinity and biological evolution—a pattern of death and new life, of self-sacrificial love that results in new forms of life. We are called to give up our little egos in order to join the divine cosmic dance of sacrifice and new life.[43]

Reading Christian theology and biological evolution together as a process of self-emptying offers a way of understanding our posture within the life of the Earth. McFague asserts, "To see the sharing of basic resources

---

37. McFague, *New Climate for Christology*, xi.
38. McFague, *New Climate for Christology*, 11.
39. McFague, *New Climate for Christology*, xiii.
40. McFague, *New Climate for Christology*, 6.
41. McFague, *New Climate for Christology*, 19.
42. McFague, *New Climate for Christology*, 51.
43. McFague, *New Climate for Christology*, 42.

as a kenotic act in our time of climate change, with its consequences of dire inequality, is an essential commitment for us."[44] Self-emptying, then, is an act of discipleship. McFague says, "Jesus and his disciples must expend themselves, giving simply not from their excess but from the very marrow of their bones."[45] If we look to Jesus' self-emptying as a model for discipleship, then "Jesus reveals not a mighty Lord but a self-expending friend."[46] McFague sees friendship as an important way for interpreting our self-emptying relationship with the Earth. She says, "Friends are 'inside' the dance (including human beings), engaging as partners in the greatest show of all time—the evolution of planet earth," and "the cosmic dance encourages all friends to give and take through the strange activity of self-sacrifice for others."[47] Humans are not lords over the Earth, but rather, friends who empty themselves for their friends, following the model of Jesus' self-emptying. "Perhaps," McFague says, "we can assume a more humble position for ourselves on earth, not claiming we know everything or can fix everything, but listening to those who spend many years studying an event, as well as 'listening' to the planet itself."[48]

A homiletics of entanglement that follows insights from postcolonial praxis and moves toward an ecohomiletics will emerge with a posture of self-emptying humility and open-ended listening with the cry of the Earth.

POSTCOLONIAL ECOTHEOLOGY: CULTIVATING A CRITICAL CONSCIOUSNESS

Environmental catastrophe summons the attention and transformation of every preacher. While the positions and relations of preachers within environmental catastrophes vary—an Anglo-American female preacher in a suburb of Atlanta and a Puerto Rican male preacher in Tijuana will experience environmental catastrophes differently—their urgency should persist with passion and resolve. The importance of ecological theology for preaching, at this point in human history, should be beyond debate.

---

44. McFague, *New Climate for Christology*, 72.
45. McFague, *New Climate for Christology*, 76.
46. McFague, *New Climate for Christology*, 80.
47. McFague, *New Climate for Christology*, 83.
48. McFague, *New Climate for Christology*, 94.

Searching for Speech

The Earth radiates the glory of God and teaches the preacher how to feel, think, relate, and speak in such a time as this.[49] Witnessing smog, polluted rivers, extracted minerals, desolate landscapes, species extinctions, and extreme weather, the preacher feels and listens with the sighing and groaning of the Earth's vast unraveling. The preacher stands as witness to the Earth's plundered splendor. The speech of a preacher as a witness arises from the genius of the Earth's biodiverse life, of which a preacher is but a part. Most fundamentally, the preacher learns from the Earth what needs to be said. The Anthropocene—"the human dominated epoch" arising from industrial and neocolonial projects—is an occasion and context for interpreting the tasks of preachers.

While an Anglo-American ecological theologian, preacher, or church leader may have no qualms following guidance from an environmentalist such as John Muir and speaking eloquently about our entanglement with the biodiverse life of the Earth, the same ecological theologian, preacher, or church leader may practice little critical awareness for their relationship with the history of their source material or the history of the land on which they stand. They may practice little critical awareness for John Muir's racism or for the conservation movement's displacement of Native peoples.[50] I have found myself liable of this in my theology and preaching, residing comfortably within imperial freedom and cultural erasure, unquestioningly benefiting from militarism and land theft. While Sallie McFague's writings have been instrumental in my life and in the development of the present work, I question why McFague lifts up someone such as Muir as a "good naturalist" to follow.[51] Why is he the touchstone for cultivating observational techniques for ecological theology? Why not suggest following observational techniques from someone such as Robin Wall Kimmerer? Our models are important because they shape and animate our praxis. The biases and allegiances of our models will often infect our praxis.

On the one hand, I have gladly followed Muir and similar Eurocentric voices as authoritative and poetic sources for my sermons, and I have lauded the conservation movement's achievements. On the other hand, I have sought to follow guidance from Native and postcolonial history,

---

49. Mayra Rivera asserts, "The glory of God shines in the bodies of all created beings as a sign of their participation in God." *Touch of Transcendence*, 139.

50. Dina Gilio-Whitaker notes, "Instrumental in the creation of Yosemite National Park, [John Muir] supported the expulsion of the Yosemite Indians from their ancient home in the valley." *As Long as Grass Grows*, 100.

51. McFague, *New Climate for Christology*, 67.

spirituality, and praxis. Yet, my practice of one has not fully touched upon my practice of the other. Put another way, I have not fully reckoned with a postcolonial critique of ecological theology, environmental justice, and conservation. While ecological theology and postcolonial praxis share overlapping concerns for environmental catastrophe, they also share substantive areas of tension and even contradiction. Ecological theology and postcolonial praxis share a concern for *place*, but ecological theology and postcolonial praxis also share areas of significant divergence. Whereas ecological theology may focus on the conservation of a place from a Eurocentric perspective and with little concern for Native peoples or immigration, postcolonial praxis focuses on violent displacement from a place by colonial or neocolonial projects and with substantial concern for causes underlying violent displacement and forced immigration. Concern for the conservation of places should not be separate from concern for the violent displacement of peoples from places.

Postcolonial criticism and praxis can deliver well-intentioned ecological theology and homiletics from historical and moral ineptitude. Postcolonial criticism and praxis offer ecological theology and homiletics a useful critique and deeper critical awareness for source material and the histories that have brought us into the land on which we stand. Our relations constitute who we are—"I am because we are," including all biodiverse life. Breaking from the confines of Eurocentric and Anglo-American ecological theology and following insights from the liberating energies of postcolonial criticism means questioning and expanding our relations and ongoing possibilities. It means assessing encounters with the Other in which the Other is touched but not grasped and which call into question the circumstances under which the Other has become designated as "Other"[52]—the designation of "Third World" for example potentially conceals the circumstances under which the "Third World" has been formulated.[53] These encounters

---

52. Rivera, *Touch of Transcendence*, 2, 42, 103, 106.

53. Several notes for preachers using general designations are in order. Mayra Rivera observes, "Certain people become strangers; not only do we identify them as such, but we develop social, political, and economic structures in which they are defined as strangers. Similarly, through our repeated use of signifiers like 'Third World,' for instance, we inscribe categories of difference in the world and then allow ourselves to forget the range of forces that went into their production." *Touch of Transcendence*, 105. Anglo-American Christians in the United States may gaze upon Haiti and render it as a "Third World" country without comprehending the history of European colonization that has violently and actively prevented Haitian people from growing in political and economic strength. Kwok Pui-Lan, however, observes the continuing importance of such designation, as she

and critiques with the Other do not unfold from a single or even multiple positions. Rather, these encounters and critiques are unsettled, provisional, and ongoing. Gayatri Chakravorty Spivak observes, "I always attempt to look around the corner, to see ourselves as others would see us."[54]

During a visit to Friendship Park in Tijuana, as the sun was setting over the Pacific and lights were shining across the city, a friend of Border Church asked us, "What is the church in America doing? Do they care we are here?" He asked the questions as we looked through the border fence and saw the bright lights of San Diego. I did not have a response. As a pastor of a church in San Diego, I could have told him stories about the committee meetings I attend or the donations people make or the service projects or the new worshipping communities or the college ministry but that was not what he was inquiring about. His questions disclosed an unanswered question: "Is the church in America reckoning with how the rest of the world sees the church in America?" Such questions challenge us to look around the corner and to look at ourselves from where other people see us as we continue to occupy unceded lands.

When Mayra Rivera observes, "As we touch one another, we are in touch with a multitude,"[55] she foregrounds the immensity of encounter that cannot be ever fully grasped or signified. There will always be more to question, critique, learn, and meet amidst the incalculable relations that constitute who we are as historied bodies. Each individual is more than an individual. Each moment is more than a moment—"each moment is the fruit of forty thousand years . . . every moment is a window on all time."[56]

---

notes, "Many have questioned whether the term 'Third World' still makes sense. . . . This book still uses the term 'Third World' because it connotes not simply a geographical area but the tremendous power imbalance between the powerful and the disenfranchised." *Hope Abundant*, 1. Gayatri Chakravorty Spivak suggests using the term *colonialism* for European conquests, *neocolonialism* for dominant economic, political, and cultural maneuvers in the twentieth century, and *postcoloniality* for "the contemporary global condition." *Critique of Postcolonial Reason*, 172. Kwok Pui-Lan has noted, "The prefix 'post' denotes not only a temporal period or political transition of power but also reading strategies, practices, and actions that challenge colonialism and its legacy." *Postcolonial Politics and Theology*, 10. Whether or not preachers follow such suggestions, an important feature of self-critical preaching will involve practicing an awareness of the severe limitations and histories that have formed various designations contributing to the formation of the so-called "Other."

54. Spivak, *Critique of Postcolonial Reason*, xii–xiii.
55. Rivera, *Touch of Transcendence*, 97.
56. Wolfe, *Look Homeward, Angel*, 5.

Toward a Homiletics of Entanglement

There will always be another corner to look around, another angle to center, another ungraspable meeting of possibilities. Ivone Gebara comments, "We are not guided by a single, normative model or paradigm, whether it be in culture, in our way of living our Christianity, or in our sexual orientation. . . . There is no one model or criterion for determining what is authentic knowing."[57] No singular narrative or model will be sufficient for understanding and articulating our encounters with one another and the lands we occupy. "We are trying," as Gebara says, "to decentralize our power to possess and dominate in order to build new meanings based on relatedness, independence, and universal brotherhood/sisterhood."[58] For those of us residing comfortably within imperial freedom, land theft, and cultural erasure, in legacies of colonization and whiteness—especially for men residing comfortably within these legacies—postcolonial praxis and criticism in dialogue with ecological theology will invite us into choosing a humbler path for preaching, moving men, the West, and Christian ecclesiastical structures and doctrines from a theological center.

With attention to social, political, religious, economic, geographic, biodiverse, cultural, and textual entanglements of globalized life, a homiletics of entanglement learns from the Earth what needs to be said and employs a postcolonial critique of ecological theology and homiletics.[59] A homiletics of entanglement breaks from the confines of Eurocentric ecological theology and follows insights from the liberating energies of postcolonial praxis and criticism. A homiletics of entanglement moves toward decentering white androcentric ecological preaching.[60] Cultivating a critical consciousness in relation with the unceded lands we occupy will be an ongoing task of a homiletics of entanglement, both for the

---

57. Gebara, *Longing for Running Water*, 64.

58. Gebara, *Longing for Running Water*, 115.

59. While postcolonial preaching may find useful insights from ecological theology, here, I am turning the critical mirror on ecological theology. Ecological theology has much to learn from postcolonial criticism. Postcolonial criticism and ecological theology can enter into a dialectical relationship.

60. John McClure describes what he terms "other-wise preaching," which is "other-inspired and other-directed," "toward the stranger," a "homiletics under deconstructive erasure so that preaching might be transformed." *Other-Wise Preaching*, xi. Decentering ecological preaching with a homiletics of entanglement, however, will not begin from the center and move "toward the stranger," as McClure recommends. Rather, decentering ecological preaching will involve *beginning* in places and with people who are not centered by Anglo-American male experience.

Anglo-American female preacher in a suburb of Atlanta and the Puerto Rican male preacher in Tijuana.

BIOMIMICRY: LEARNING FROM THE GENIUS OF THE EARTH

A homiletics of entanglement will listen, learn, and imitate biodiverse community. "Biomimicry," a term described by Janine Benyus, values the wisdom of the Earth's life. With biomimicry, Benyus outlines biodiverse life as model, measure, and mentor. She characterizes biomimicry as "the conscious emulation of life's genius. Innovation inspired by nature."[61] Rather than exploring the Earth for what can be extracted, biomimicry looks to the Earth for what can be learned. The Earth has had billions of years to test what works and what can be sustained. We can learn from the genius of the Earth's life. Benyus explains, "The more our world looks and functions like this natural world, the more likely we are to be accepted on this home that is ours, but not ours alone."[62] Many fields of research are practicing biomimicry. Benyus observes, "[Biomimics] are fascinating people, working at the edges of their disciplines in the fertile crests between intellectual habitats. Where ecology meets agriculture, medicine, material science, energy, computing, and commerce, they are learning that there is more to discover than to invent. They know that nature, imaginative by necessity, has already solved the problems we are struggling to solve. Our challenge is to take these time-tested ideas and echo them in our own lives."[63]

With a desire to develop ways to sustainably produce food, Wes Jackson, the director of the Land Institute, asserts, "How do we act on the fact that we are more ignorant than we are knowledgeable? Embrace the arrangements that have shaken down in the long evolutionary process and try to mimic them, every mindful that human cleverness must remain subordinate to nature's wisdom."[64] Given the fact that "topsoil is essentially nonrenewable,"[65] Jackson has observed, "Essentially, we have to farm the

---

61. Benyus, *Biomimicry*, 2.
62. Benyus, *Biomimicry*, 3.
63. Benyus, *Biomimicry*, 4.
64. Benyus, *Biomimicry*, 11.
65. Benyus, *Biomimicry*, 14.

way nature farms,"[66] which involves "learning the secrets of a prairie."[67] At the Land Institute, they are seeking to learn from the Earth's time-tested genius in order to better understand how to produce food sustainably. The Earth is their model, measure, and mentor.

Janine Benyus also explores the possibility of "industrial ecology" that conducts "business the way a sun-soaked hickory forest recycles its leaves."[68] Could trees teach businesses how to conduct business? "The basic tenet of industrial ecology," Benyus explains, "says that we should try, wherever possible, to work only with substances that nature would recognize and assimilate."[69] Industrial ecology seeks to mimic Earth's economy. Instead of extracting resources from poor countries and dumping waste in low-income communities, an industrial ecology would use local resources and recycle waste as an energy source. "We have to learn to be self-renewing right where we are," Benyus says.[70] What if trees were a model, measure, and mentor for corporate businesses and emerging technologies?

A homiletics of entanglement will subvert the hubris of anthropocentrism by imitating and learning from biodiverse community. A homiletics of entanglement will listen with humility to the Earth as model, measure, and mentor.

Biomimicry in the preaching event can be simple. In a sermon entitled "Small is Beautiful," I preached on Jesus' parable of the mustard seed[71] and the way in which the kingdom of heaven mimics not apex predators but rather mimics the behavior of trees. After the worship service, I provided seeds that are native to San Diego and invited church leaders—elders and deacons—to plant the seeds in small bowls and to take them home. I welcomed them into the slow and fragile process of cultivation. The sermon was then not only a thought experiment for their attention in the sanctuary during the formal worship service; the sermon entered into their homes and the attention of their daily lives. What are the implications of the kingdom of heaven mimicking small seeds and trees? In what ways would our preaching change if the life of trees was our guide? In what ways would a

---

66. Benyus, *Biomimicry*, 21.
67. Benyus, *Biomimicry*, 26.
68. Benyus, *Biomimicry*, 239.
69. Benyus, *Biomimicry*, 240.
70. Benyus, *Biomimicry*, 251.
71. Matthew 13:31–32.

church's life change if the life of trees rather than a capitalistic business was the icon and model for a church's life?

Biomimicry can be playful.[72] In a sermon entitled "Discovering Beautiful Entanglements," I preached on a text in Ezekiel,[73] and I invited the congregation to practice a lighthearted form of biomimicry by wearing black and yellow antennae with the appearance of bumblebees. Laughter rippled through the congregation as serious adults donned the black and yellow antennae.[74] Ezekiel envisioned God transplanting the tip of a cedar tree onto a high mountain. The tiny cedar transplant will grow, flourish, and provide fruit and shelter. As the cedar grows, it will provide nourishment and a home to every kind of bird and every kind of "winged creature." The tree will be an ecosystem. In the sermon, I wondered with the congregation whether Ezekiel could have included bees in the trees' branches when he envisioned every "winged creature" in the tree. At that point in the sermon, the congregation was part of the preaching event, and I took it as an opportunity to reflect on the importance of bees in the life of many ecosystems—how can we learn from the life of bees? While I knew that later in the summer we would be building beehives together as part of the church's music and arts camp, I did not imagine that later in the summer we would save bees on our church campus and that women's church groups would invite guest speakers to offer educational seminars on the importance of bees. In what ways can such playful biomimicry bring the life of bees into the church's collective awareness and affection?

Biomimicry may lead us into questions we otherwise would not have imagined. An ongoing question for preachers may be, "In what ways can preaching gesture toward and even embody biomimicry?" Anna Lowenhaupt Tsing reflects on the smell of matsutake mushrooms. Smell can be a powerful conduit of memory. Tsing comments, "Smell draws us into

---

72. Joseph M. Webb has asserted, "The comic persona is not contradictory to the gospel; in fact, the gospel itself needs comic personas in order for its speaking to be both inviting and invigorating. For those who have both the courage and sensitivity to bring the spirit of play and playfulness into the pulpit, the rewards, to both the church and the gospel will be remarkable indeed." *Comedy and Preaching,* 137, as cited by Myers, *Stand-Up Preaching,* 56.

73. Ezekiel 17:22–24.

74. Jacob D. Myers argues that the comical can "foster the condition of possibility for seeing the world differently," and he says, it "can lead us to reflect upon—and even question—our ideologies." *Stand-Up Preaching,* 32.

entangled threads of memory and possibility."⁷⁵ Matsutake mushrooms emit a distinct smell that brings joy for those who love the mushroom and associate fond memories with it. Tsing notes, "When Koreans expanded to Japan in the eighth century, they cut down forests. Pine forests sprung up from the deforestation, and with them matsutake. Koreans smelled the matsutake—they thought of home."⁷⁶ If preachers explore ways of embodying biomimicry and consider the power of smell for evoking memories, preachers may consider a question such as, "What is the smell of a sermon?" Asking such a question may seem absurd. Yet, asking such a question can uncover hidden assumptions about what a sermon is and does, and such a question may raise fresh trajectories for homiletical biomimicry.

COLLECTIVE EFFERVESCENCE: MOVING TOGETHER WITH THE EARTH

A homiletics of entanglement will join in the life of many forms of life in multiple directions. "Collective effervescence," a term coined by Émile Durkheim, describes the "electric exaltation of moving together."⁷⁷ When humans participate in coordinated movements, their biological rhythms synchronize. Humans can actually feel themselves joining a collective experience. Dacher Keltner notes, "Sports' fans heart rhythms synchronize when they watch games together, their collective pulse tracking the agonies and ecstasies of the game,"⁷⁸ and other such community events that involve unison movement can create this experience of physiological synchronicity, such as funerals, graduations, and group walking.⁷⁹ Emotions can be contagious. Keltner observes, "Cricket teammates whose laughter and joy spread to one another bat better in ensuing innings on the pitch."⁸⁰ People's bodies are connected with synchronized physical movement.

The experience of collective effervescence has origins in ancient human cultures. Keltner explains, "When European colonists first traveled to Africa, they were awestruck, and more often horrified, by the dances of the people they encountered. Dance's pervasiveness, effervescence, and

---

75. Tsing, *Mushroom at the End of the World*, 45.
76. Tsing, *Mushroom at the End of the World*, 49.
77. Keltner, *Awe*, 95–96.
78. Keltner, *Awe*, 99.
79. Keltner, *Awe*, 101–5.
80. Keltner, *Awe*, 111.

power unnerved these Westerners seeking fortunes and to 'save souls.' In Africa, communities danced to appreciate childbirth, puberty, weddings, and death, moving people into a shared understanding of the cycle of life."[81] European colonists failed to comprehend what they were witnessing. They failed to perceive that the unison movements of dance reinforced the community's values. "In Africa, and many Indigenous cultures worldwide, dance was and often still is a physical, symbolic language of awe."[82] The dances tell their community's stories.

Humans can also learn collective effervescence by observing other species. Keltner explains, "Successful groups move in unison and integrate different talents into a smoothly functioning, synchronized whole," and he continues, "One of the most successful species on the planet, the leafcutter ant, puts the varying skills of its different members to use in a coordinated whole: there are leaf cutters, haulers, builders—all cutting leaves, transporting them, building their home, tending to the queen."[83] The ants move in unison, each contributing toward the collective well-being of the group.

James Bridle notes the ways in which honeybees make decisions in highly organized synchronicity and equality. Bridle explains, "Honeybees present us with one of the greatest spectacles of animal communication and democracy-in-practice, known as the 'waggle dance.' This is the process by which they share information about nearby pollen sources and make decisions about new nesting sites."[84] Karl von Frisch learned that the honeybees were not using the "waggle dance" only to communicate excitement at having discovered a food source. The dance was actually conveying much more complex messages, including where and how far away the food source was located.[85] More research revealed that the honeybees' dances were not only communicating the location of food sources; they were also making decisions as a group and expressing political preferences. "In short," Bridle explains, "bees partake in a kind of direct democracy—as practiced in such diverse human settings as ancient Athens, the Paris Commune, the cantons of Switzerland, Quaker meetings, the Kurdish, Arab and Assyrian self-administration of Rojava, and Citizens' Assemblies."[86] Their dances are

---

81. Keltner, *Awe*, 113.
82. Keltner, *Awe*, 113.
83. Keltner, *Awe*, 111–12.
84. Bridle, *Ways of Being*, 258–59.
85. Bridle, *Ways of Being*, 259.
86. Bridle, *Ways of Being*, 261–62.

forms of communication and political decision-making. Could the highly organized form of group communication among honeybees also be a way they experience collective effervescence?

If a homiletics of entanglement aims at creating a collective, performative event, in what ways can the preaching event facilitate and promote collective effervescence? A homiletics of entanglement will move beyond a monologue behind a pulpit or on a stage and move into a multidirectional, dialogical, and embodied event. A homiletics of entanglement will gather biodiverse community into shared experience. Such moves will likely require changes in the arrangement of liturgical and homiletical space. Moreover, does the preaching event always unfold within a walled and roofed space? Does the event ever unfold outdoors? Such moves will require preachers to unlearn homiletical habits, assumptions, and etiquette.

Promoting collective effervescence can take the form of simple gestures that invite the congregation into a shared performative event. When I preached the sermon "Discovering Beautiful Entanglements" on a text in Ezekiel,[87] I did not only invite the congregation to practice a playful form of biomimicry. I invited the congregation to practice playful biomimicry *together*. It became a collective experience with shared laughter and reflection. They were experiencing collective effervescence, and the sermon created the occasion of collective effervescence. The collective effervescence event has now been etched into the congregation's shared memory and identity. Can such playful forms of biomimicry and collective effervescence promote feelings of kinship between species?

POLYPHONIES: ATTUNING WITH VOICES OF THE EARTH

A homiletics of entanglement will be attuned to polyphonies of sound, not only attuned to sounds of human languages and cultures, but of languages and cultures of multiple species. Whole landscapes and territories of sound will unfold before a preacher and spiritual community. Vinciane Despret invites attention be given to the multifaceted character of the singing of birds. What can preachers learn from being attentive to the fields of sound birds create?

Outside of her bedroom window, Despret noticed a blackbird's song. She began to notice that there was more to the bird's song than an

---

87. Ezekiel 17:22–24.

enthusiastic repetition. This led Despret to explore the meanings and significances of the songs of birds. Birds create whole territories and interact with territories through their songs. "A territory," she explains, "is a place where all sorts of things and events are played out in a different way—where ways of doing things, ways of being, are opened up to other connections, to other assemblages," and she continues, "Territory is a place where everything becomes rhythm, melodic landscape, motifs and counterpoints, matters of expression."[88] Territories of sound and rhythm are not created for only a single reason or use. Her observations regarding the creation of melodic territories have caused me to wonder what sorts of territories we create with the unfolding of the preaching event. If spaces are formed in part through sound, then what sorts of spaces or sanctuaries are we forming with sermons?

Despret asks, "Have you ever traveled by train with headphones on? Have you felt, as has often been my own experience, that the passing landscape could be 'Bach-like' or 'Tchaikovsky-like', or sensed to what extent music imprints itself, covers and affects our surroundings? An accordion in the metro can change not only our mood but even our way of perceiving things."[89] Sound can change our experience of a space. Despret says, "The bird's song will therefore be expressive power," and "*the bird's song becomes one with the space.*"[90] Can a sermon be an extension of a preacher and can a sermon be an expressive mode of a sanctuary just as a territory created by a bird's song is an extension of the bird's body and a shaping performance of a territory? If a sermon does act as an extension of a preacher and a shaping of a sanctuary, then what is being extended and shaped?

Though a bird's song is an extension of a bird's body and shaper of a territory, a bird's song also features information. "If a bird's song," Despret says, "has become the expression of a place, no doubt she will recognize in its signature the height of trees, the presence of a neighborhood, whether peaceful or noisy . . . the rough texture of rocks, the presence of a spring with a song of its own, the shade canopy, the taste of its fruits or of insects under the leaves, and perhaps even the way sunlight filters through foliage."[91]

---

88. Despret, *Living as a Bird*, 89, 94.
89. Despret, *Living as a Bird*, 106.
90. Despret, *Living as a Bird*, 107.
91. Despret, *Living as a Bird*, 109.

Toward a Homiletics of Entanglement

A bird's song does not only extend one's body, shape territory, and disseminate information about the territory. A bird's song shares proximity and even joins in the songs of other birds. Despret asks, "Why is there this apparent desire for proximity among birds?"[92] In part they share information, but they also have other reasons. Despret observes, "Living together synchronizes reproductive cycles" and affords opportunities to participate in an "acoustic collective."[93] Could birds be experiencing collective effervescence and not only that but also collective effervescence between species of birds? Despret notes, "There are sometimes exchanges, 'captures', entanglements that are far more complex than a simple and ostensibly relatively indifferent juxtaposition."[94] A study in Central Italy showed that "interspecific choruses do indeed exist."[95] The researchers showed that "when the overlapping songs occupy the same frequency range, the singers were observed to adjust vocal production on a very short temporal scale. There is therefore neither cacophony nor intervals of silence but, instead, a score made up of different parts and reprises. These choruses are therefore evidence of genuine coordination."[96] Multiple species of birds sing together.

Might preachers and spiritual communities learn from multiplicities of species of birds who sing in chorus together? A homiletics of entanglement may explore ways of creating polyphonic events by forming spaces for voices of the human and the more-than-human. In the unfolding preaching event, what are the territories of sound and how can those territories be occasions of joining across species?[97] Are the territories of sound limited to human voices? Are the territories of sound limited to a single human gender and language and culture? In what ways can the territories of sound be opened and multiplied? In what ways can the preaching event open a preacher and spiritual community to multiplicities of territories of sound, bearing witness to the proclamation of the glory of God in all the Earth? All the Earth is proclaiming the glory of God—are we lifting every voice and affirming polyphonies of proclamation? As we learn from the chorus of

---

92. Despret, *Living as a Bird*, 123.
93. Despret, *Living as a Bird*, 124, 146–47.
94. Despret, *Living as a Bird*, 152.
95. Despret, *Living as a Bird*, 156.
96. Despret, *Living as a Bird*, 158.
97. Stevie Wonder experimented with polyphonies across multiple species on his album *Journey through the Secret Life of Plants* in 1979.

birds, will we also be attentive to them for their own sake, for their intrinsic value,[98] lest they become only a mirror for our own learning?

"If the earth groans and creaks," Despret says, "it also sings . . . but [these songs] will disappear all the more rapidly if we do not pay attention to them. And with them will also disappear a multiplicity of different ways of inhabiting the earth, of the inventiveness of life, of arrangements, melodic scores, fragile appropriations, ways of being, things that matter. . . . What we risk losing, because of our failure to pay attention, will be the courageous singing of birds."[99] The beauty and complexity of birds' singing is an invitation to attentiveness. Birds embody yet another way of inhabiting territories, forming spaces, and joining with the songs of the Earth. "Salvation," Rubem Alves said, "is the recovery of the polyphony of life."[100]

CONCLUSIONS: FINDING OUR PLACE(S) WITHIN THE EARTH

Larry Rasmussen asserts, "Until we enter the places of suffering and experience them with those who are entangled there, as God does, our actions will not be co-redemptive."[101] Whether we are dwelling in the open wound of the borderland or entering into deforested landscapes where birds no longer sing, "to care is to learn how to be entangled," as Cláudio Carvalhaes has said.[102] Preachers must enter and learn how to be entangled in the places of suffering, and we will only ever move *toward* a homiletics of entanglement because such a homiletical approach will only ever be local, provisional, and ongoing.

What if preaching preparation and the preaching event arise from the daily entanglements of life? What if the exegesis of a biblical text moves into the interpretation of geographic space and the geographic space moves into the exegesis of a biblical text?[103] What if the many connections and en-

---

98. McFague, *Body of God*, 165.
99. Despret, *Living as a Bird*, 160–61.
100. Alves, *Poet, the Warrior, the Prophet*, 128.
101. Rasmussen, *Earth Community, Earth Ethics*, 286.
102. Carvalhaes, *How Do We Become Green People and Earth Communities?*, 112.
103. McFague observes, "Geography . . . may well be *the* subject of the twenty-first century. Where is the best land and who controls it? How much good space is left and who is caring for it? Justice for those on the underside, whether these be human beings or other vulnerable species, has everything to do with space." *Body of God*, 101–2.

counters with biodiverse life in the course of a week animate the unfolding of the sermon on a Sunday morning?[104] What if foraging were to become a spiritual practice and part of sermon preparation in the slow process of learning *how* to be entangled with a place?[105]

Expanding upon Kwok Pui-Lan's insights for postcolonial preaching—privileging marginalized voices, preaching as a performative event, drawing from the community's diversity—a homiletics of entanglement privileges the marginalized voices of the Earth through biomimicry, creates preaching as a performative event with collective effervescence, and draws from the community's biodiversity by listening with polyphonies of voices. A homiletics of entanglement honors insights from postcolonial preaching and turns toward and arises from the life of the Earth in conversation with biblical texts.

Ecotheology traces connections across all forms of knowledge and relationships in biodiverse community. Ecotheology understands humans as within the life of the Earth, and particularly, ecotheology offers a humbler posture for humans' relationship within the Earth. Spiritual community can follow the model of the self-emptying Trinity revealed in the self-emptying life of Jesus. In addition to the self-emptying of material resources, spiritual communities can practice self-emptying of anthropocentric hubris by befriending the Earth as a model, measure, and mentor for what is appropriate. In these ways, a homiletics of entanglement can move toward an ecohomiletics by embodying the self-emptying dance of the Trinity and biological evolution.

Following aforementioned insights, a homiletics of entanglement that moves toward an ecohomiletics will be attentive to ways in which the exploitation of labor, land, and landfills target the most vulnerable populations of the human and the more than human. A homiletics of entanglement will be attentive to ways in which the relationships of forests, the lives of insects, the biodiversity of rainforests, and the vibrancy of rural human communities are being decimated.

---

104. McClure encourages preachers "to bring their pre-sermonic reflection into the largest possible conversation." *Other-Wise Preaching*, 60. McClure describes conversation with the human congregation. Could this "largest possible conversation" potentially include interspecies encounter?

105. The first time I went foraging for *gosari* roots and *dureup* shoots I was visiting my wife's side of the family in the countryside of Korea. It was a profoundly beautiful experience and a reminder to me of what generations of families have needed to do and continue to do in order to survive.

Preaching preparation and the preaching event should exit the confined rooms of monologues and enter the spacious ecosystems of multidirectional dialogues. As we learn from the life of the Earth, join in collective experience, and attune ourselves to many voices, we will enter the pathos of biodiverse life, feeling the longings and the fulfillments of the Earth. Our hearts may learn that pathos speaks louder than words. A homiletics of entanglement will be a homiletics of many, ongoing transformations. A homiletics of entanglement will not merely encourage environmentalism and environmentally focused sermon content. Rather, a homiletics of entanglement will bring preachers and spiritual communities to see and feel themselves as within the life of the Earth. A homiletics of entanglement will be fundamentally ecological, following and tracing encounters and connections across the cultural, economic, political, biological, and social fields of connection. This is a multidisciplinary theory and practice for sermon preparation and for the preaching event.

Learning *how* to be entangled in life-giving and life-affirming ways can be a process of experimentation for preparing and for preaching sermons. To subvert anthropocentrism, what are ways we can imitate the life of the Earth in the unfolding act and event of preaching? What are ways we can invite listeners into collective participation in the preaching event? What are ways we can lift every voice and sing with a fuller appreciation for our biodiverse community's polyphonic life? These are open-ended questions with numerous responses and embodiments that will vary by local community.

My search for speech has led me to realize that gospel speech amidst the Anthropocene arises from transformed living. Such speech arises from living in ways that feel, think, relate, touch, and walk lightly and gently with all beings and forms of life. No amount of environmental data profusion from the pulpit will be sufficient. But when our speech arises from our own transformed living, then our speech may become gospel speech for us and for the ecosystems in which we belong. Gospel speech arises from a transformation of every preacher.[106]

I have often wondered whether there can there be a gospel found in the Western world, whether there can be a gospel for the Western world. If there is a possibility of a gospel in, for, from, and with the Western

---

106. Karl Barth asserted, "The homiletic art is to speak about the present, about experience, about the new life that has happened in history, but it may not do so except with a thrust toward tomorrow. We are a people that walk in darkness. But we have seen a great light." *Homiletics*, 55.

Toward a Homiletics of Entanglement

world, it must be predicated on the lamentation, confession, repentance, and transformation of the Western world.[107] The same Western European colonization that has racialized the world has plundered the Earth. Western, Eurocentric theology and homiletics will need to undergo complete transformation.

As we find ourselves entangled with biodiverse life, we will not gaze upon "nature" as a reality "out there," separate from ourselves. Rather, we will find ourselves within the life of the Earth. The Earth's life will no longer be a commodity to exploit for our voracious consumption. The Earth's life will be part of us and we will be part of the Earth's life.

PROMPTS FOR PREACHING PREPARATION— CATALOGUING EMBODIED ENTANGLEMENTS

When you read a biblical text, observe and consider the more-than-human life in the text. In what ways do the more-than-humans play an active role in the biblical text?

Since humans depends on the tangle of biodiverse life in order to live, experiment with centering a more-than-human subject in your sermon preparation and sermon message.

Record in a notebook your experiences with the full range of your senses to embrace and feel the tangle of more-than-human life "here."

Sink your hands in the soil.

Touch the bark of a tree with your fingertips; notice the bark's color and texture.

Witness the cascading tangles of light you.

Catalogue the wounded splendor.

Listen to the feast of sound.

---

107. Justo L. González and Catherine G. González have observed that in the biblical text, "God has a proclivity for speaking the word through the powerless. The whole Bible bears witness to this. Is this an accident, or is it an essential element of the gospel itself? Is there something about God's word that can best be heard and spoken by the powerless? We would say there is indeed," and they continue, "The powerless have a more ready access to an authentic understanding of the gospel than do the powerful. The powerful need to hear the word through voices they have rejected in their own society." *Liberating Pulpit*, 21.

Searching for Speech

"Discovering Beautiful Entanglements"[108]

Ezekiel 17:22–24

The prophet Ezekiel draws a picture of a tree and birds and winged creatures of every kind sharing a beautifully entangled life, each one contributing to the other one's life. This is what I want us to ponder today: living a beautifully entangled life.

At the beginning of 2018, James Bridle, an artist and author, was invited to give a talk at a big, glossy event in Vancouver. The topic of the talk was to be some of the gloomier aspects of the internet, and particularly the effects of online video and algorithms on children.

As a speaker at the conference, Bridle was offered a range of "regional experiences," which included a tour of the redwood forests on the city's edge, led by a biologist from the University of British Columbia. So, James climbed into the bus with a couple dozen other attendees and went for a walk in the woods.

Their guide was professor Suzanne Simard, who had spent decades studying redwood forests on Canada's Pacific coast. As they walked among the mossy trunks, Suzanne explained to the group how huge trees were intimately connected to one another with underground networks of fungi. Trees are selective in whom they choose to help: mother trees favor their own offspring, sending more carbon to them than to unrelated seedlings, and shifting their roots to make room for them to grow. Mother trees, however, are not selfish. Through underground networks of fungi, the trees will go to the aid of other species of trees in times of need. In the summer, the shaded fir trees receive much-needed carbon and sugar from the taller birch trees, while in autumn the fir trees return the favor as birch trees start to lose their leaves. The trees, even of different species, help each other through these underground networks of fungi.

But, as Bridle went on this tour with professor Suzanne Simard, he learned that not only were the trees intimately connected to one another through underground networks of fungi, they were also connected to places far outside the forest itself. For example, a significant proportion of the essential nitrogen that the trees and other forest plants take up through their

---

108. With many worshippers in the congregation wearing black and yellow bee antennae, including children and adults, I preached this sermon on June 4, 2023, at Faith Presbyterian Church, San Diego. I was also wearing black and yellow bee antennae at the beginning of the sermon.

roots is ultimately derived from the middle of the Pacific Ocean, thousands of miles away. There is a particular nitrogen isotope called nitrogen-15 that is much more common in marine algae than in most land vegetation. Yet it is found in surprising amounts in coastal forests. So how does it get from the depths of the ocean to the forest? The way the nitrogen-15 gets from the marine algae to the coast forest is absolutely marvelous. The fish that feed on the algae in the deep ocean become enriched with nitrogen-15. One of these fish is the Pacific salmon, which every year returns to spawn in the same rivers and streams from which they have hatched, on the coast of the western United States and Canada. So, as the Pacific salmon make the perilous trip home, many of them will invariably become fertilizer for the trees. The fish quite literally bring the nitrogen from the ocean that the trees need to thrive. The fish feed the trees, and the trees create the habitat for the salmon to spawn.

After this whirlwind tour with Suzanne Simard exploring the ways in which trees, fish, algae, and fungi are all networked together, James Bridle climbed back into the bus and returned to the conference to talk about technology, the internet, and the modern networks that seem to have replaced, or at least drowned out, the underground networks of the forest.[109]

So much of the vibrant life around us and within us is caught up in awe-inspiring entanglement, if we slow down to notice.

In today's Old Testament Scripture reading, the prophet Ezekiel envisions God transplanting the tip of a cedar tree onto a high mountain. The tiny cedar transplant will grow, flourish, and provide fruit and shelter. As the cedar grows, it will provide nourishment and a home to every kind of bird and every kind of winged creature. It will be an ecosystem. We might suppose that the prophet Ezekiel is using an easily relatable image from the Earth's life in order to talk about Israel's relationship with God and with the surrounding nations. That is, God will plant and grow Israel into a tree under which all the peoples of the Earth can flourish.

In the sixth century, many of the Israelites were taken off into exile by the Babylonian empire. Ezekiel was with them in exile. So, now, we may suppose, Ezekiel gives them this vision as a kind of story to remind them that it is not Egypt or Babylon that is their source of life. Rather, it is God, who makes the trees rise and fall, who is their source of life. And, it is God who will plant them and help them thrive. And in their thriving, all the peoples of the earth will thrive also.

109. Bridle, *Ways of Being*, 59–61.

That is a fine, acceptable reading of the prophet Ezekiel's vision. But, what if we slow down and take more seriously the image of the tree, offering nourishment and shelter and life-affirming relationships. What if we take this image more seriously, not merely as a *metaphor* but rather as a *model* for our community life, which has God as its source?

The biologist Janine Benyus expands upon the term *biomimicry*. Benyus says biomimicry is "the conscious emulation of life's genius." In other words, Benyus explains, "People who make our world, the designers and the engineers and the architects and the construction workers, when they go to solve a problem, they say, 'What in the natural world has already solved this problem?' And then they try to imitate that organism or that ecosystem and hopefully come up with something that helps us live here more gracefully."[110]

So, not only in a metaphorical sense, but also in a very literal sense, we humans copy nature all the time, with our technology and with our forms of relating. You may think of solar panels. You may think of forthcoming wetlands in Mission Bay, San Diego. You may also think of the ways in which wastewater engineers mimic the membrane in oceans that filter salt water. And what is the internet but a copy of networks of trees connected by fungi?

In various ways with our technologies and relationships, we humans copy nature all the time, because we are part of nature. We have something to learn from the intimate and mutual relationships within nature, and Ezekiel's vision is an invitation to take nature more seriously as a model for our community life.

The prophet Ezekiel envisions the tree being a home to every winged creature. I wonder if "every winged creature" in the tree's branches includes bees. Yes, I think it would. The world is home to more than 20,000 species of bees. Two of the most common hole-nesting bee species used for crop pollination are alfalfa leafcutter bees and blue mason bees. In the wild, both species nest in pre-made holes, such as old grub tunnels, crevices in peeling bark, or broken branches. So, yes, pollinator bees live in trees. As suggested by their names, leafcutter bees use pieces of leaves to build their nests, while mason bees use mud or clay.

Some reports indicate that nearly 40 percent of bees are facing extinction today, so many people have been wondering what they can do to help. One thing you can do is to start locally, in your own backyard. Making your

---

110. Benyus, "Biomimicry, an Operating Manual for Earthlings."

garden as bee-friendly as possible is as easy as adding things like native wildflowers and native bee nesting sites, including bee houses.

While honeybees have their place, it is bees such as leafcutter bees and mason bees that are critical to growing food and flowers.[111] That is the beauty of bees. They are spreading grace all over the place, and much of the time, it is unintentional. Think about it. They are searching for nectar, and they are spreading pollen.

What if, for a moment, we draw inspiration from the prophet Ezekiel, and we create our own community model inspired from the life of nature? What if we practice biomimicry, imitating the genius of nature? We may not be the great cedar of Israel. Perhaps, we could choose a humbler model for ourselves to imitate. What if we choose a pollinator garden as our model to imitate for our community life? A pollinator garden includes a mixture of plants and even wildflowers. Every flower, every blade of grass, every bee, every butterfly, every hummingbird, every dandelion, every person contributes to the vibrancy and life of the pollinator garden. The pollinator garden is entangled in nearly countless forms of life. And, the pollinator garden can be more than a *metaphor* for us. The pollinator garden can be a *model* of life, a model of beautiful entanglements. So, if we accept a pollinator garden as a *model* for our church, then cross-pollination will be important for the life the of the pollinator garden church. In every direction, pollinator bees will look for signs of nectar and pollen.

So, here is your mission. You are pollinator bees. This church is a pollinator garden. Your mission is to look for signs of nectar and of pollen, to look for signs of possibility in every direction. This church needs you to cross-pollinate within this garden and with the surrounding gardens. The preschool is part of this garden. Look for signs of possibility in your relationship with the preschool. You may not think you have a relationship with the preschool. I beg to differ. Consider your experience in education, with children, with food, with gift-giving, with storytelling. Consider cross-pollinating with the preschool. The university is a garden next to us. Look for signs of possibility in your daily routines and your daily relationships with the university. You may not think you have a relationship with the university. I beg to differ. Consider your experience with education, with students, with life experience, with food, with storytelling. Consider cross-pollinating with the university. Begin with a single relationship. The surrounding neighborhood is the wider meadow, with trees and wildflowers

---

111. Burnett, "Native Bees."

interrelated and all over the place. Look for signs of possibility in your daily life within this neighborhood or your neighborhood, if you live in a different neighborhood.

As you move about in your neighborhood, slow down and notice who crosses your path, who crosses your daily routine—your local park and grocery store and school and bus stop and theater and restaurant.

Look for nectar and spread some pollen. And start small. Offer a simple gesture of kindness that gives life to a person or people who cross your path. Or, if you notice a creature other than a human, offer a simple gesture of kindness to a hummingbird or a kitten who crosses your path.

If anyone asks you what your heard at church today, you can say, "Well, I thought I was a human, but I discovered I am a pollinator bee." As a pollinator bee, you may be searching for nectar, but remember to slow down long enough to spread some pollen.

Even, perhaps in small ways, your job is to spread life across the preschool, university, and your neighborhood, to the people and places you cross, to spread life across the human and the more-than-human.

Cross-pollination goes both ways. When you take life out into these other gardens, you will naturally bring life from these other gardens into this one. The life of this pollinator garden depends on cross-pollination, depends on each of us searching for and pursuing signs of possibility. Bring life into every beautiful entanglement so that, as Ezekiel says, every kind of bird, every winged creature, every person will find shelter and nourishment.

The church is our pollinator garden.

You are pollinator bees.

And, remember, bees are spreading grace all over the place, and much of the time, it is unintentional.

That is your mission.

Bring life into every beautiful entanglement in which you find yourself.

Show video: "What a Wonderful World," by Jon Batiste.

Conclusion
Friendship in the Garden

> "I have told you that Kafka speaks
> of the messenger who cannot deliver
> his message. But what of the messenger
> who *does* deliver his message,
> but nothing changes?"[1]
>
> ELIE WIESEL

> "A stone sits in my stomach because
> I know that Anthropocene citizens
> who continue Holocene habits
> doom their children."[2]
>
> LARRY L. RASMUSSEN

ON OUR WALKS TO his elementary school, Ezra emphatically instructs me not to step on snails, and I remind him to listen to the birds' songs. Each of us is reminding the other to pay attention. Ezra and I are each other's disciples of attention and tenderness. The Earth is alive beyond what our imaginations can hold—a single acre of soil from a temperate zone carries about 125 million invertebrates.[3] We are friends with so many creatures—or at least we are in the process of becoming friends. I confess I have accidentally stepped on a snail occasionally, to Ezra's utter shock and dismay. We both hear the crunch underneath my shoe. I immediately feel terrible.

---

1. Burger, *Witness*, 194.
2. Rasmussen, *Planet You Inherit*, 12.
3. Rasmussen, *Earth Community Earth Ethics*, 264.

"How could you do that?" he asks, coming to a standstill. I will then usually mumble, still waking up with coffee in hand, "I really did not intend to do that," acknowledging my carelessness and inattention. How we treat smaller creatures reveals our character.[4] I am still learning to walk lightly. Those of us who are raising children in the Anthropocene are still unlearning careless habits carried from the Holocene. I am slowly learning to participate in what Thomas Berry called "the Great Work," to "carry out the transition from a period of human devastation of the Earth to a period when humans would be present to the planet in a mutually beneficial manner."[5]

When I began writing this book, I thought the subject was "preaching" and especially the "historical positioning of a preacher." Since finishing this book and grappling with my craft of preaching, all the while seeking to be ever more attentive to my place within the life of the Earth, I have found myself continuing to struggle with whether an increased number of ecologically focused sermons will make a positive difference in the life of churches. What if nothing changes in our congregations, though we dedicate ourselves completely to ecohomiletics? At the midway point of writing this book, I began to realize that the subject was the "preacher," and more specifically "me." This book is about my ongoing journey of transformation as a preacher, who is searching for a deeper relationship with the Earth. I often return to what Cláudio Carvalhaes told me years ago: "Unless you are transformed, no one around you will be transformed." It is not only the preacher's speech that must be transformed. It is also the preacher who must be transformed. I began this journey searching for transformed speech. I began hoping and searching for powerful words and ways of speaking that would change the people and communities around me. In my search for powerful speech, I have changed. I am no longer looking only for words, but rather, I am searching for forms of relating tenderly with trees, rivers, mountains, and creatures great and small. I am no longer preaching to the equivalent of stuffed animals; full-bodied animals and trees are preaching to me. I am continuing this journey as an ongoing personal transformation, and my words arise from this search. Preachers live by metaphors. I hope,

---

4. Tsing, Deger, Saxena, and Zhou describe "friendly farming" in Taiwan, in which young people in the countryside refuse to use molluscicides and instead carefully hand-pick snails off of rice seedlings, even composing songs, telling stories, and instituting festivals in the snails' honor. The snail is an icon of their political platform, arguing that another world is possible. *Field Guide to the Patchy Anthropocene*, 142.

5. Berry, *Great Work*, 3.

CONCLUSION

with this book, I have offered useful metaphors that invite a deeper, more entangled relationship with the Earth—"theology as poetic gardening."[6]

No sermon is ever entirely finished. It is in the living that a sermon finds its truest and fullest completion—"sermons are living things."[7] If preachers are akin to trees, what if our sermons behave as mycelium between trees, receiving life and giving life in many different directions all at once? The Spirit of Life creates generative connections the preacher may never have foreseen or intended. I have found this to be true in my experience as I seek not only to transform my speech but also to transform my life in relationship with the Earth. I am continuing to search for ways of speaking and relating, of receiving and of giving life. The sermons included here embody a glimpse of growth in my ongoing journey of transformation as a preacher and my experimentations with preaching during the Anthropocene.

As a preacher, I want to acknowledge publicly that our world has changed, and we should not continue reading the Bible and practicing our faith as if our lives intersect with the Bible in the same ways as preachers in the sixteenth or even twentieth centuries. The human population has grown exponentially. The planet teeters on the brink, and many people in the Western world wish only to continue consumption as if the Earth's life exists merely for our voracious plundering. As a preacher, I want to embody another way that cherishes the life of the Earth and bears witness to our life as residing within the many entanglements of the Earth's life. I can live differently, and I can share my experience. I can offer invitations into communal experimentation that touch the Earth lightly. As a preacher, I want to conspire with churches in forming alliances across many traditions and organizations to promote biodiverse well-being. Doctrinal and cultural differences need not keep us apart. We can learn from ancient wisdom other than our own in Christian traditions, wisdom that has arisen from love for the land and wisdom of the land. When we learn from these wisdoms, we will find gospel in our hearts and on our lips.

The times in which we live are overwhelming. None of us can untangle the Anthropocene's devastating contradictions alone, and we do not have to. Preachers can begin a journey of transformation with their congregations. The summer after I preached a series of sermons entitled, "A Greener Faith," our congregation in San Diego built beehives, which were

---

6. Alves, *Poet, the Warrior, the Prophet*, 131.
7. Carvalhaes, *What's Worship Got to Do with It?*, 198.

given to beekeeping families in Mexicali. In the same month that we built the beehives, San Diego declared itself a Bee City, committed to creating pollinator-friendly spaces across the city. Women's groups in the church also invited guest speakers to conduct educational seminars about the life and importance of bees. In the same week their guest speakers visited, I donned a beekeeper costume in order to move a beehive from the church's preschool playground so a professional beekeeper could later and appropriately relocate the beehive. I had not realized that we would spend a year together becoming tenderly entangled with the lives of bees. One moment led to another, like cross-pollination. I find deep encouragement in witnessing people dedicate their lives to healing our relationship with the Earth. I also find myself encouraged when people open themselves to new possibilities and forms of relationship. I love being in spiritual community, and I am committed to a life of preaching. All of us can be on a journey of transformation together, and as we practice ways of relating tenderly, learning how to be entangled with the Earth's life will continue to animate our search for speech.

Bibliography

Aeschliman, Gordon. "Loving the Earth is Loving the Poor." In *The Green Bible, Introduction*, 91–97. New York: HarperCollins, 2008.

Alper, Becka A. "How Religion Intersects with Americans' Views on the Environment: Responsibility for the Earth is part of U.S. Christians' beliefs, but so is skepticism about climate change." Pew Research Center, November 17, 2022. https://www.pewresearch.org/religion/2022/11/17/how-religion-intersects-with-americans-views-on-the-environment/.

Alves, Rubem A. *The Poet, the Warrior, the Prophet*. London: SCM, 1990.

Augustine. *On Christian Doctrine*. Translated by J. F. Shaw. Mineola, NY: Dover, 2009.

Barth, Karl. *Homiletics*. Louisville: Westminster John Knox, 1991.

Bass, Diana Butler. *Grounded: Finding God in the World: A Spiritual Revolution*. New York: HarperCollins, 2017.

Beckert, Sven, and Seth Rockman. *Slavery's Capitalism: A New History of American Economic Development*. Philadelphia: University of Pennsylvania Press, 2016.

Benyus, Janine M. *Biomimicry: Innovation Inspired by Nature*. New York: HarperCollins, 1997.

———. "Biomimicry, an Operating Manual for Earthlings." *On Being*, March 23, 2023. https://onbeing.org/programs/janine-benyus-biomimicry-an-operating-manual-for-earthlings/.

Berry, Thomas. *The Great Work: Our Way into the Future*. New York: Three Rivers, 1999.

Berry, Wendell. *The Unsettling of America: Culture and Agriculture*. Berkeley, CA: Counterpoint, 2015.

———. *What Are People For? Essays*. Berkeley: Counterpoint, 2010.

Block, Melissa. "She Ripped up Her Manicured Lawn." *NPR*, May 5, 2023. https://www.npr.org/2023/05/05/1172727763/garden-gardening-book-writing-soil-dungy.

Boff, Leonardo. *Cry of the Earth, Cry of the Poor*. Maryknoll, NY: Orbis, 2002.

———. *Thoughts and Dreams of an Old Theologian*. Maryknoll, NY: Orbis, 2022.

Boyle, Gregory. *Forgive Everyone Everything*. Chicago: Loyola, 2022.

Bridle, James. *Ways of Being: Animals, Plants, Machines: The Search for a Planetary Intelligence*. London: Farrar, Straus and Giroux, 2022.

Brueggemann, Walter. *Finally Comes the Poet: Daring Speech for Proclamation*. Minneapolis: Fortress, 1989.

———. *The Prophetic Imagination*. Philadelphia: Fortress, 1985.

———. "Trees: Signals of Hope and Defiance." Church Anew, April 6, 2023. https://churchanew.org/brueggemann/trees-signals-of-hope-and-defiance.

Bibliography

Burger, Ariel. *Witness: Lessons from Elie Wiesel's Classroom.* Boston: Mariner, 2019.

Burnett, Christopher. "Native Bees: The Best Pollinators for Your Garden." Almanac.com, May 24, 2023. https://www.almanac.com/native-bees-best-pollinators-your-garden.

Carvalhaes, Cláudio. *How Do We Become Green People and Earth Communities? Inventory, Metamorphoses, and Emergenc(i)es.* New York: Barber's Son, 2022.

———. *Ritual at World's End: Essays on Eco-Liturgical Liberation Theology.* New York: Barber's Son, 2021.

———. *What's Worship Got to Do with It? Interpreting Life Liturgically.* Eugene, OR: Cascade, 2018.

Clark, Seth. *Church at the Wall: Stories of Hope along the San Diego-Tijuana Border.* King of Prussia, PA: Judson, 2022.

Codington, Sam. *Listening as Hosts: Liturgically Facing Colonization and White Supremacy.* Eugene, OR: Cascade, 2024.

Craddock, Fred B. *Preaching.* Nashville: Abingdon, 1985.

Davis, Ellen F. "Knowing Our Place on Earth: Learning Environmental Responsibility from the Old Testament." In *The Green Bible, Introduction*, 58–64. New York: HarperCollins, 2008.

DeLoughrey, Elizabeth M. *Allegories of the Anthropocene.* Durham, NC: Duke University Press, 2019.

Despret, Vinciane. *Living as a Bird.* Cambridge: Polity, 2022.

Figueres, Christiana, and Tom Rivett-Carnac. *The Future We Choose: The Stubborn Optimist's Guide to the Climate Crisis.* New York: Vintage, 2021.

Francis, Pope. *Laudato Si': On Care for Our Common Home.* Vatican City: Vatican, 2015.

Gaventa, Beverly Roberts. *When In Romans: An Invitation to Linger with the Gospel according to Paul.* Grand Rapids: Baker Academic, 2016.

Gebara, Ivone. *Longing for Running Water: Ecofeminism and Liberation.* Minneapolis: Fortress, 1999.

Gilio-Whitaker, Dina. *As Long as Grass Grows: The Indigenous Fight for Environmental Justice, from Colonization to Standing Rock.* Boston: Beacon, 2020.

González, Justo L., and Catherine G. González. *The Liberating Pulpit.* Nashville: Abingdon, 1994.

Graeber, David, and David Wengrow. *The Dawn of Everything: A New History of Humanity.* London: Farrar, Straus and Giroux, 2021.

Gutierrez, Gustavo. *We Drink from Our Own Wells: The Spiritual Journey of a People.* Maryknoll, NY: Orbis, 1992.

Hạnh, Thích Nhất. *Love Letter to the Earth.* Berkeley: Parallax, 2013.

Hick, John. *Evil and the Love of God.* New York: Harper & Row, 1966.

Jennings, Willie James. *The Christian Imagination: Theology and the Origins of Race.* New Haven: Yale University Press, 2010.

Jewett, Robert. *Romans.* Minneapolis: Fortress, 2007.

Johnson, Ayana Elizabeth, and Katharine K. Wilkinson. *All We Can Save: Truth, Courage, and Solutions for the Climate Crisis.* New York: One World, 2021.

Kara, Siddharth. *Cobalt Red: How the Blood of the Congo Powers Our Lives.* New York: St. Martin's, 2023.

———. *Modern Slavery: A Global Perspective.* New York: Columbia University Press, 2023.

Keltner, Dacher. *Awe: The New Science of Everyday Wonder and How It Can Transform Your Life.* New York: Penguin, 2023.

Bibliography

Kim-Cragg, HyeRan. *Postcolonial Preaching: Creating a Ripple Effect.* Lanham, MD: Lexington, 2021.

Kimmerer, Robin Wall. *Braiding Sweetgrass: Indigenous Wisdom, Scientific Knowledge, and the Teaching of Plants.* Minneapolis: Milkweed, 2013.

Kolbert, Elizabeth. *The Sixth Extinction: An Unnatural History.* New York: Picador, 2015.

Kopenawa, Davi. *The Falling Sky: Words of a Yanomami Shaman.* Cambridge, MA: Belknap, 2023.

Kwok, Pui-Lan. *Hope Abundant: Third World and Indigenous Women's Theology.* Maryknoll, NY: Orbis, 2013.

———. *Postcolonial Politics and Theology: Unraveling Empire for a Global World.* Louisville: Westminster John Knox, 2021.

Lefteri, Christy. *The Beekeeper of Aleppo: A Novel.* New York: Ballantine, 2020.

Limburg, James. *Hosea to Micah.* Louisville: Westminster John Knox, 2011.

Long, Thomas G. *The Witness of Preaching.* 2nd ed. Louisville: Westminster John Knox, 2005.

Lowry, Eugene L. *How to Preach a Parable: Designs for Narrative Sermons.* Nashville: Abingdon, 1989.

Lunetta, Caleb. "What Killed 3 Million Honey Bees in North County? Beekeepers Fear the Answer Has Larger Ramifications." *The San Diego Union Tribune,* October 14, 2023.

Maathai, Wangari. *Unbowed: A Memoir.* New York: Anchor, 2007.

McCarthy, Michael. *The Moth Snowstorm: Nature and Joy.* New York: New York Review, 2018.

McClure, John S. *Other-Wise Preaching: A Postmodern Ethic for Homiletics.* St. Louis: Chalice, 2001.

McFague, Sallie. *The Body of God: An Ecological Theology.* Minneapolis: Fortress, 1993.

———. *A New Climate for Christology: Kenosis, Climate Change, and Befriending Nature.* Minneapolis: Fortress, 2021.

Mendoza, Alexandra. "Protestors Chain Themselves to Border Wall in Tijuana in Opposition to New Construction." *The San Diego Union Tribune,* October 26, 2023.

Mendoza, S. Lily, and George Zahariah. *Decolonizing Ecotheology: Indigenous and Subaltern Challenges.* Eugene, OR: Pickwick, 2022.

Merton, Thomas. "The Merton Prayer." In *Reflections,* Spring 2012. https://reflections.yale.edu/article/seize-day-vocation-calling-work/merton.prayer.

———. *Thoughts in Solitude.* New York: Farrar, Straus and Giroux, 1999.

Mitchell, Sherri Weh'na Ha'mu Kwasset. "Indigenous Prophecy and Mother Earth." In *All We Can Save,* edited by Ayana Elizabeth Johnson and Katharine K. Wilkinson, 16-28. New York: One World, 2021.

Moltmann, Jürgen. *The Spirit of Life: A Universal Affirmation.* Minneapolis: Fortress, 2001.

Moss, Otis III. *Blue Note Preaching in a Post-Soul World: Finding Hope in an Age of Despair.* Louisville: Westminster John Knox, 2015.

Myers, Jacob D. *Stand-Up Preaching: Homiletical Insights from Contemporary Comedians.* Eugene, OR: Cascade, 2022.

Nixon, Rob. *Slow Violence and the Environmentalism of the Poor.* Cambridge: Harvard University Press, 2013.

Ó Tuama, Pádraig. *In the Shelter: Finding a Home in the World.* London: Hodder & Stoughton, 2015.

Powers, Richard. *The Overstory: A Novel.* New York: W. W. Norton & Company, 2019.

Bibliography

Powery, Luke A. *Becoming Human: The Holy Spirit and the Rhetoric of Race.* Louisville: Westminster John Knox, 2022.

Presbyterian Mission. "Intersectional Priority: Climate Change." https://web.archive.org/web/20230527183250/https://www.presbyterianmission.org/ministries/matthew-25/intersectional-priority-climate-change/.

Rasmussen, Larry L. *Earth Community Earth Ethics.* Maryknoll, NY: Orbis, 1997.

———. *Earth-Honoring Faith: Religious Ethics in a New Key.* New York: Oxford, 2013.

———. *The Planet You Inherit: Letters to My Grandchildren When Uncertainty's a Sure Thing.* Minneapolis: Broadleaf, 2022.

Rivera, Mayra. *The Touch of Transcendence: A Postcolonial Theology of God.* Louisville: Westminster John Knox, 2007.

Said, Edward W. *Orientalism.* New York: Vintage, 1979.

Schade, Leah D. *Creation-Crisis Preaching: Ecology, Theology, and the Pulpit.* St. Louis: Chalice, 2015.

Schweitzer, Albert. *Reverence for Life.* New York: Harper & Row, 1969.

Sheldrake, Merlin. *Entangled Life: How Fungi Make Our Worlds, Change Our Minds, and Shape Our Futures.* New York: Random House, 2021.

Simard, Suzanne. *Finding the Mother Tree: Discovering the Wisdom of the Forest.* New York: Vintage, 2022.

Sleeth, J. Matthew. "The Power of a Green God." In *The Green Bible, Introduction,* 17–24. New York: HarperCollins, 2008.

Smith, Linda Tuhiwai. *Decolonizing Methodologies: Research and Indigenous Peoples.* 3rd ed. New York: Bloomsbury Academic, 2022.

Smith, Mitzi J., and Young Suk Kim. *Toward Decentering the New Testament: A Reintroduction.* Eugene, OR: Cascade, 2018.

Spivak, Gayatri Chakravorty. *A Critique of Postcolonial Reason: Toward a History of the Vanishing Present.* Cambridge: Harvard University Press, 1999.

Stancil, Joanna Mounce. "The Power of One Tree—The Very Air We Breathe." US Department of Agriculture, March 17, 2015. https://www.usda.gov/about-usda/blog/power-of-one-tree-very-air-we-breathe.

Stuart, Douglas. *Hosea to Jonah.* Grand Rapids: Zondervan, 2014.

Taylor, Dorceta E. *Toxic Communities: Environmental Racism, Industrial Pollution, and Residential Mobility.* New York: New York University Press, 2014.

Thurman, Howard. "The Sound of the Genuine." Baccalaureate Ceremony at Spelman College, May 4, 1980. https://thurman.pitts.emory.edu/items/show/838.

Tsing, Anna Lowenhaupt. *The Mushroom at the End of the World: On the Possibility of Life in Capitalist Ruins.* Princeton: Princeton University Press, 2015.

Tsing, A., J. Deger, A. Saxena, and F. Zhou. *Field Guide to the Patchy Anthropocene: The New Nature.* Stanford, CA: Stanford University Press, 2024.

Whyte, David. *Everything is Waiting for You.* Langley, WA: Many Rivers, 2003.

Wilson, E. O. *The Creation: An Appeal to Save Life on Earth.* New York: W. W. Norton & Company, 2007.

Wohlleben, Peter. *The Hidden Life of Trees: What They Feel, How They Communicate.* Berkeley: Greystone, 2016.

Wolfe, Thomas. *Look Homeward, Angel.* New York: Scribner, 2006.

Wright, N. T. *Paul: In Fresh Perspective.* Minneapolis: Fortress, 2009.

Yong, Ed. *I Contain Multitudes: The Microbes Within Us and a Grander View of Life.* New York: Ecco, 2018.

www.ingramcontent.com/pod-product-compliance
Lightning Source LLC
Chambersburg PA
CBHW031503160426
43195CB00010BB/1094